THE WAR AND UNITY

THE WAR AND UNITY

BEING LECTURES DELIVERED AT THE
LOCAL LECTURES SUMMER MEETING OF
THE UNIVERSITY OF CAMBRIDGE, 1918

EDITED BY THE REV.

D. H. S. CRANAGE, Litt.D.

KING'S COLLEGE

CAMBRIDGE
AT THE UNIVERSITY PRESS
1919

CAMBRIDGE
UNIVERSITY PRESS

University Printing House, Cambridge CB2 8BS, United Kingdom

Published in the United States of America by Cambridge University Press, New York

Cambridge University Press is part of the University of Cambridge.

It furthers the University's mission by disseminating knowledge in the pursuit of
education, learning and research at the highest international levels of excellence.

www.cambridge.org
Information on this title: www.cambridge.org/9781107651241

© Cambridge University Press 1919

First published 1919
First paperback edition 2014

A catalogue record for this publication is available from the British Library

ISBN 978-1-107-65124-1 Paperback

PREFACE

FOR some time past the Local Examinations and Lectures Syndicate have arranged a Summer Meeting in Cambridge every other year in connexion with the Local Lectures. The scheme of study has always included a number of theological lectures, and at the last two meetings an attempt has been made to deal with some of the religious and moral problems suggested by the War. In 1916 a course of lectures was delivered, and afterwards published by the University Press, on *The Elements of Pain and Conflict in Human Life*. In 1918 the Syndicate decided to arrange a course on Unity. It was at first suggested that the lectures should be confined to the subject of Christian Reunion, but it was finally arranged to deal not only with Unity between Christian Denominations, but with Unity between Classes, Unity in the Empire, and Unity between Nations.

Many of those who attended expressed a strong wish that the lectures should be published, and the Lecturers and the Syndicate have cordially agreed to their request. The central idea of the course is undeniably vital at the present time, and the book is now issued in the hope that it may be of some help in the period of "reconstruction."

D. H. S. CRANAGE,

Secretary of the Cambridge University
Local Lectures.

November 1918.

CONTENTS

UNITY BETWEEN CHRISTIAN DENOMINATIONS

UNITY BETWEEN CLASSES

UNITY BETWEEN CHRISTIAN DENOMINATIONS

I. A GENERAL VIEW

By the Rev. V. H. Stanton, D.D.

The governing idea of this early morning course, which at the present as at former Summer Meetings is devoted to a subject connected with religious belief, is this year the power that Christianity has, or is fitted to have, to unite Christian denominations with one another, and also to unite races and nations, and different portions of that commonwealth of nations which we call the British Empire, and different classes within our own nation. A moment's reflection will shew that the question of unity between denominations of Christians derives special significance from being placed in connexion with all those other cases in regard to which the promotion of unity is to be considered. If it belongs to the genius of Christianity to be a uniting power, it is above all in the sphere of professed and organised Christianity, where Christians are grouped together *as* Christians, that its influence in producing union should be shewn. If it fails in this here, what hope, it may well be asked, can there be that it should be effective, when its principles and motives cannot be applied with the same directness and force? In the very assumption, then, which underlies this whole course of lectures, that Christianity can unite men, we have a special reason for considering our relations to one another as members of Christian bodies, with regard to this matter of unity.

But we are also all of us aware that the divisions among Christians are often severely commented on by those who refuse to make any definite profession of the Christian Religion, and are given by them sometimes as a ground of their own position of aloofness. It is true that strictures passed on the Christian Religion and its professors for failures in this, as well as in other respects, frequently shew little discernment, and are more or less unjust. So far as they are made to reflect on Christianity itself, allowance is not made for the nature of the human material upon which and with which the Christian Faith and Divine Grace have to work. And when Christians of the present day are treated as if they were to blame for them, sufficient account is not taken of the long and complex history, and the working of motives, partly good as well as bad, through which Christendom has been brought to its present divided condition. Still we cannot afford to disregard the hindrance to the progress of the Christian Faith and Christian Life among men created by the existing divisions among Christians. Harm is caused by them in another way of which we may be, perhaps, less conscious. They bring loss to ourselves individually within the denominations to which we severally belong. We should gain incalculably from the strengthening of our faith through a wider fellowship with those who share it, the greater volume of evidence for the reality of spiritual things which would thus be brought before us; and from the enrichment of our spiritual knowledge and life through closer acquaintance with a

variety of types of Christian character and experience;
and not least from that moral training which is to be
obtained through common action, in proportion to the
effort that has to be made in order to understand the
point of view of others, and the suppression of mere
egoism that is involved.

These are strong reasons for aiming at Christian unity.
But further there comes to all of us at this time a powerful incentive to reflection on the subject, and to such
endeavours to further it as we can make, in the signs of
a movement towards it, the greater prominence which
the subject has assumed in the thought of Christians, the
evidence of more fervent aspirations after it, the clearer
recognition of the injury caused by divisions. I remember
that some 40 or more years ago, one of the most eminent
and justly esteemed preachers of the day defended the
existence of many denominations among Christians on
the ground that through their competition a larger
amount of work for the advance of the kingdom of God
is accomplished. We are not so much in love with competition and its effects in any sphere now. And it should
always have been perceived that, whatever its rightful
place in the economic sphere might be, it had none in
the promotion of purely moral and spiritual ends. The
preacher to whom I have alluded did not stand alone in
his view, though perhaps it was not often so frankly
expressed. But at least acquiescence in the existence of
separated bodies of Christians, as a thing inevitable, was
commoner than it is now.

In the new attitude to this question of the duty of
unity that has appeared amongst us there lies an opportunity which we must beware of neglecting. It is a move-

ment of the Spirit to which it behoves us to respond energetically, or it will subside. Shakespeare had no doubt a different kind of human enterprises mainly in view when he wrote:

> There is a tide in the affairs of men,
> Which taken at the flood, leads on to fortune;
> Omitted, all the voyage of their life
> Is bound in shallows and in miseries.

But this observation is broadly true of all human progress. An advance of some kind in the relations of men to one another, or the remedying of some abuse, begins to be urged here and there, and for a time those who urge it are but little listened to. Then almost suddenly (as it seems) the minds of many, one hardly knows why, become occupied with it. If in the generation when that happens desire leads to concentrated effort, the good of which men have been granted the vision in their minds and souls will be attained. Otherwise interest in it will pass away, and the hope of securing it, at least for a long time, will be lost.

Before we attempt to consider any of the problems presented by the actual state of Christendom in connexion with the subject now before us, let us go back in thought to the position of believers in Jesus Christ of the first generation, when His own brief earthly life had ended. They form a fellowship bound together by faith in their common Lord, by the confident hopes with which that faith has inspired them, and the new view of life and its duties which they have acquired. Soon indeed instances occur in which the bonds between different members of the body become strained, owing especially to differences of origin and character in the elements of

which it was composed. We have an example at a very
early point in the narrative of the book of *Acts* in the
dissatisfaction felt by believers from among Hellenistic
Jews, who were visiting, or had again taken up their
abode at, Jerusalem, because a fair share of the alms was
not assigned to their poor by the Palestinian believers,
who had the advantage of being more permanently established in the city, and were probably the majority. But
the chiefs among the brethren, the Apostles, take wise
measures to remove the grievance and prevent a breach.

A few years later a far more serious difference arises.
Jewish believers in Jesus had continued to observe the
Mosaic Law. When converts from among the Gentiles
began to come in the question presented itself, "Is observ-
ance of that Law to be required of them?" Only on condition that it was would many among the Jewish believers
associate with them. In their eyes still all men who did
not conform to the chief precepts of this Law were
unclean. It is possible that there were Jews of liberal
tendencies, men who had long lived among Gentiles, to
whom this difficulty may have seemed capable of settlement by some compromise. But in the case of most Jews,
not merely in Palestine, but probably also in the Jewish
settlements scattered through the Græco-Roman world,
religious scruples, ingrained through the instruction they
had received and the habits they had formed from child-
hood, were deeply offended by the very notion of joining
in common meals with Gentiles, unless they had fulfilled
the same conditions as full proselytes to Judaism, the so-
called "proselytes of righteousness." On behalf, however,
of Gentiles who had adopted the Faith of Christ, it was
felt that the demand for the fulfilment of this condition

of fellowship must be resisted at once and to the utter-most. So St Paul held. To concede it would have caused intolerable interference with Gentile liberty, and hin-drance to the progress of the preaching of the Gospel and its acceptance in the world. And further—upon this consideration St Paul insisted above all—the requirement that Gentiles should keep the Jewish Law might be taken to imply, and would certainly encourage, an entirely mistaken view of what was morally and spiritually of chief importance; it would put the emphasis wrongly in regard to that which was essential in order that man might be in a right relation to God and in the way of salvation.

But the point in the history of this early controversy to which I desire in connexion with our present subject to draw attention is the fact that it is not suggested from any side that Jewish Christians and Gentile Christians should form two separate bodies that would exist side by side in the many cities where both classes were to be found, keeping to their respective spheres, endeavouring to behave amicably to one another, "agreeing to differ" as the saying is. This would have been the plan, we may (I think) suppose, which would have seemed the best to that worldly wisdom, which is so often seen to be folly when long and broad views of history are taken. And we can imagine that not a few of the ecclesiastical leaders of recent centuries might have proposed it, if they had been there to do so. For never, perhaps, have there been more natural reasons for separation than might have been found in those national and racial differences, and in those incompatibilities due to previous training and associa-tions between Christians of Jewish and Gentile origin.

Yet it is assumed all through that they *must* combine. And St Paul is not only sure himself that to this end Jewish prejudices must be overcome, but he is able to persuade the elder Apostles of this, as also James who presided over the believers at Jerusalem, though they had been slower than he to perceive what vital principles were at stake. Believers of both classes must join in the Christian Agapæ, or love-feasts, and must partake of the same Eucharist, because the many are one loaf[1], one body. They must grasp, and give practical effect to, the principle that "there is neither Jew nor Greek, neither bond nor free, neither male nor female, for all are one in Christ Jesus[2]."

For that society, or organism, into which Jewish and Gentile believers were alike brought, a name was found; it was that of *Ecclesia*, translated *Church*. It will be worth our while to spend a few moments on the use of this name and its significance. We find mention in the New Testament of "the Church" and of "Churches." What is the relation between the singular term and the plural historically, and what did the distinction import? The sublime passages concerning the Church as the Body of Christ and the Bride of Christ occur in the Epp. to the Colossians and Ephesians[3], which are not among the early Pauline Epistles. Nevertheless in comparatively early Epistles, the authorship of which by St Paul himself is rarely disputed, there are expressions which seem plainly to shew that he thought of the Church as a single body to which all who had been baptized in the Name of Jesus Christ belonged. In the Epp. to the Galatians and

[1] 1 Cor. x. 17, R.V. mg. [2] Gal. iii. 28.
[3] Col. i. 18, 24; Eph. i. 22, v. 23 ff.

1 Corinthians[1] he refers to the fact that he persecuted the "Church of God," and his persecution was not confined to believers in Jerusalem or even in Judæa, but extended to adjacent regions. He might have spoken of "the Churches of Syria," as he does elsewhere (using the plural) of those of Judæa, Galatia, Asia, Macedonia[2]. But he prefers to speak of the Church, and he describes it as "the Church of God." The impiety of his action thus appeared in its true light. He had not merely attacked certain local associations, but that sacred body—"the Church of God." Again, it is evident that he is thinking of a society embracing believers everywhere when he writes to the Corinthians concerning different forms of ministry, "God placed some in the Church, first Apostles, secondarily prophets" and so forth[3]. Again, when he bids the Corinthians, "Give no occasion of stumbling, either to Jews or to Greeks, or to the Church of God[4]," or asks them whether they "despise the Church of God[5]," although it was their conduct to brethren among whom they lived that was especially in question, it is evident that, as in the case of his own action as a persecutor, the gravity of the fault can in his view only be truly measured when it is realised that each individual Church is a representative of the Church Universal. This representative character of local Churches also appears in the expression common in his Epistles, the "Church in " such and such a place.

The usage of St Paul's Epistles does not, therefore, encourage the idea that the application of the term *ecclesia* to particular associations preceded its application

---

[1] Gal. i. 13; 1 Cor. xv. 9.
[2] 1 Cor. xvi. 1, 19; 2 Cor. viii. 1; Gal. i. 2, 22.
[3] 1 Cor. xii. 28.   [4] 1 Cor. x. 32.   [5] 1 Cor. xi. 22.

to the whole body, but the contrary, and plainly it expressed for him from the first a most sublime conception. I may add that there is no reason to suppose that the use of the term originated with him. We find it in the Gospel according to St Matthew, the Epistle of St James and the Apocalypse of St John, writings which shew no trace of his influence.

There is no passage of the New Testament from which it is possible to infer clearly the idea which underlay its application to believers in Jesus Christ. But when it is considered how full of the Old Testament the minds of the first generation of Christians were, it must appear to be in every way most probable that the word *ecclesia* suggested itself because it is the one most frequently employed in the Greek translation of the Old Testament (the Septuagint) to render the Hebrew word kāhāl, the chief term used for the assembly of Israel in the presence of God, gathered together in such a manner and for such purposes as forced them to realise their distinctive existence as a people, and their peculiar relation to God. The believers in Jesus now formed the *ecclesia* of God, the true Israel, which in one sense was a continuation of the old and yet had taken its place. This was the view put forward by Dr Hort in his lectures on the Christian Ecclesia[1], and it is at the present time widely, I believe I may say generally, held. I may mention that the eminent German Church historians, A. Harnack[2] and Sohm[3], give it without hesitation as the true one.

Among the Jews the thought of the people in its rela-

---

[1] *The Christian Ecclesia*, pp. 3 ff.
[2] *Die Mission u. Ausbreitung d. Christentums*, p. 292.
[3] *Kirchenrecht*, I. pp. 16 ff.

tion to God was associated with great assemblies in the courts and precincts of the temple at Jerusalem, which altogether overshadowed any expression of their covenant relation to God as a people which they could find in their synagogue-worship, however greatly they valued the bonds with one another which were strengthened, and the spiritual help which they obtained, through their synagogues. But Christians had no single, central meeting-place for their common worship at which their ideal unity was embodied. It was, therefore, all the more natural that the exalted name which described that unity should be transferred to the communities in different places which shared the life, the privileges, and the responsi-bilities of the whole, and in many ways stood to those who composed them severally for the whole. The divisions between these communities were local only. They arose from the limitations to intercourse and common action which distance imposed. Or, in cases where the Church in some Christian's house is referred to, they were due to the necessity, or the great convenience, of meeting in small numbers, owing to the want of buildings for Christian worship, or the hostility of the surrounding population. Moreover these local bodies were not suffered to forget the ties which bound them all together. Those in the Greek-speaking world were required to send alms to the Churches in Judæa. Again an individual Church was not free to disregard the judgment of the rest. After St Paul has reasoned with the Corinthians on the subject of a practice which he deemed inexpedient, he clinches the matter by declaring, "we have no such custom neither the Churches of God[1]." Lastly, the Apostles, and

[1] I Cor. xi. 16.

preeminently St Paul, through their mission which, if
not world-wide, at least extended over large districts,
and the care of the Churches which they exercised, and
the authority which they claimed in the name of Christ,
and which was conceded to them, were a unifying power.

Thus the plural "the Churches" has in important
respects a different connotation in the New Testament
from that which it has in modern times. In the Apostolic
Age the distinction between the Church and the Churches
is connected only with the different degrees to which a
common life could be realised according to geographical
proximity. By a division of this nature the idea of One
Universal Church was not compromised. The local body
of Christians in point of fact rightly regarded itself as
representative of the whole body. The Christians in that
place were the Church so far as it extended there.

The preservation of unity within the Church of each
place where it was imperilled by rivalries and jealousies
and misunderstandings, such as are too apt to shew themselves when men are in close contact with one another,
and of unity between the Churches of regions remote
from one another, in which case the sense of it is likely
to be weak through want of knowledge and consequently
of sympathy—these appear as twin-aims severally pur-
sued in the manner that each required. Not indeed that
it is implied that everything is to be sacrificed to unity.
But it is demanded that the most strenuous endeavours
shall be made to maintain it, and it appears to be assumed that without any breach of it, loyalty to every
other great principle, room for the rightful exercise of
every individual gift, recognition of every aspect of
Divine truth the perception of which may be granted to

one or other member of the body, can be secured, if Christians cultivate right dispositions of mutual affection and respect.

There is one more point in regard to the idea of the Church in the New Testament as to which we must not suffer ourselves to be misled, or confused, by later conceptions and our modern habits of thought. We have become accustomed to a distinction between the Church Visible and the Church Invisible which makes of them two different entities. According to this, one man who is a member of the Church Visible may at the same time, if he is a truly spiritual person, even while here on earth belong to the Church Invisible; but another who has a place in the Church Visible has none and it may be never will have one in the Church Invisible. This conception, though it had appeared here and there before the 16th century, first obtained wide vogue then under the influence of the Protestant Reformation.

It arose through a very natural reaction from the mechanical view of membership in the Church, its conditions and privileges, which had grown up in the Middle Ages. But it does not correspond to the ideas of the Apostolic Age. According to these there is but one Church, the same as to its true being on earth as it is in heaven, one Body of Christ, composed of believers in Him who had been taken to their rest and of those still in this world. In the earlier part of the Apostolic Age the great majority were in fact still in this world. The Body was chiefly a Visible Body. It had many imperfections. Some of its members might even have no true part in it at all and require removal. But Christ Himself "sanctifies and cleanses it that He may present it"—that very same

Church—"to Himself a glorious Church, without spot or wrinkle or any such thing, but holy and without blemish[1]."

Now while one can understand the point of view from which in later times so deep a line of demarcation has been drawn between the Visible and the Invisible Church as to make of them two entirely separate things, and although to many it may still seem hard to do without this distinction, or in the existing condition of the nominally Christian world to employ that primitive conception of the Church even as, so to speak, a working hypothesis, I would ask whether the primitive conception is not a nobler and sounder one. Surely it places the ideal in its right relation to the actual. The full realisation of the ideal no doubt belongs only to another world; yet if we believe in it as an ideal we must seek to actualise it here. There is something unwholesome in acknowledging any ideal which we do not strive so far as we can to actualise. And plainly participation in the same grace, and the spiritual ties arising therefrom, ought to find expression in an outer life of fellowship, of intercourse and common action, and such common organisation as for human beings in this world these require. No doubt it is always too possible that the outward may hinder the perception of the inward. But if we can guard successfully against this danger, the inward and spiritual will become all the more potent by having the external form through which to work; while the outward, if it is too sharply dissevered in thought from the inward, loses its value and even becomes injurious.

Again, a view of the Church is more wholesome which does not encourage us to classify its members in a manner

---

[1] Ephes. v. 26, 27.

only possible to the Allseeing God; to draw a line between
true believers and others, and to determine (it may be)
on which side of the line different ones are by their
having had spiritual experiences similar to our own, and
having learned to use the same religious language that
we do; but which on the contrary leads us to think of all
as under the Heavenly Father's care, and subject to the
influences of the Holy Spirit, and placed in that Body of
Christ where, although the spiritual life in them is as
yet of very various degrees of strength,and their knowledge
of things Divine in many cases small, all may and are
intended to advance to maturity in Christ.

It is necessary that the relation of the idea of the
Church upon which I have been dwelling to her subsequent
history for centuries should be clearly apprehended. Its
hold on the minds of Christians preceded the very begin-
nings of organisation in the Christian communities, and
it would probably be no exaggeration to say that it
governed the whole evolution of that organisation for
many centuries. Particular offices were doubtless instituted and men appointed to them with specific reference
to needs which were making themselves felt. But all the
while that idea of the Church's unity and of her holiness
was present in their thoughts. And certainly as soon as it
becomes necessary to insist upon the duty of loyalty to
those who had been duly appointed to office, and directly
or indirectly to defend the institutions themselves,
appeal is made to the idea, as notably by the two chief
Christians in the Sub-Apostolic Age, Clement of Rome
and Ignatius.

It is in itself evidence of a common spirit and common
tendencies that broadly speaking the same form of con-

stitution in the local Christian communities, though not
introduced everywhere with quite equal rapidity, was
so nearly everywhere almost on the confines of the
Apostolic Age, and that soon it was everywhere. Ere long,
with this form of government as a basis, plans were
adopted expressly for the purpose of uniting the local
Churches on terms of equality among themselves, especially in combating error. And at length in the name still
of the Church's unity there came, however much we may
regret it, the centralisation of Western Christendom in
the See of Rome.

All these measures of organisation, from the earliest
to the latest of them, were means to an end; and we shall
regard them differently. But we ought not any of us to
regard means, however they may commend themselves
to us, and however sacred and dear their associations
may be, in the same way as we do the end. There must
always be the question, which will present itself in a
different light to different minds, whether particular
means, even though men may have been led by the Holy
Spirit to employ them, were intended for all time. Moreover there are points in regard to the earliest history of
Church organisation which remain obscure, in spite of
all the labour that has been expended in investigating
them: for instance the exact relation of different ministries, of the functions of different officers, to one another,
the exact moment when the orders of ministers which
proved to be permanent appeared in this or that important Church, the part which any of the immediate
disciples of Christ had in their establishment, the ideas
which at first were held as to the dependence of the rites
of the Church for their validity upon being performed

by a lawful ministry. Upon these matters, or some of them, it is possible for honest and competent inquirers to hold different opinions. But no such doubt hangs over that End which was also the Beginning, of the Church's life, that conception of what she is, or ought to be, as the society of those who confess the Name of Jesus Christ, and who are His Body. I insist upon this because I think that amid discussions on the origin of the Christian Ministry, the significance of that more fundamental question, namely, the right conception of the Christian Church, is apt to be too much lost sight of. About this, though men still do not, they ought to be able to agree, and it should be our common inspiration, both impelling us and guiding us in seeking our goal.

We need it to impel us. The obstacles to the reunion of Christendom at the present day are such that a motive which can be found is required to induce and sustain action in seeking it, whenever and wherever the opportunity for doing so presents itself; such a motive is to be found in a deep conviction of the sacredness of this object, so that our eyes may be kept fixed upon it even when there appears to be no opening through which an advance toward it can be made, and there is nothing to be done save to wait and watch and pray. But in order also that the result of any efforts that are made may be satisfactory, it is necessary that our minds should be under the guidance of a great and true idea, and that we should not simply be animated with the desire of meeting immediate needs. These are the reasons which I think justify me for having detained you so long over the consideration of the fundamental conception of the

Church which is rooted in the Christian Faith itself as it first appeared and spread in the world.

I will now, however, before concluding make a few remarks on one part of the complicated problem of reunion facing us to-day. The part of it on which I desire to speak is the relations between the Church of England, and the Churches in communion with her in various parts of the British Empire and in the United States, on the one hand, and on the other English Nonconformists, the Presbyterians of Scotland, and all English-speaking Christians allied to or resembling these. It will, I think, be generally felt that this is a part of the subject which for more than one reason specially invites our attention. There are, indeed, some, both clergy and laity, of the Church of England, though they are but a very small number in comparison with its members as a whole, whose interest in the subject of the reunion of Christendom is mainly shewn in the desire to obtain recognition for the Church of England, as a portion of the Church Catholic, from the great Church of the West. But in view of the attitude maintained by that Church there appears to be no prospect of this and nothing to be gained by attempts at negotiation. Endeavours to establish inter-communion with the Churches of Eastern Christendom may be made with more hope of success. Indeed there is reason to think that in the years to come the Church of England may be in a specially favourable position for getting into touch with these Churches and assisting them to recover from the effects of the War, and to make progress; and Englishmen generally would, I am sure, rejoice that she should undertake such work. But the question of the duty to one another of all those bodies of English

Christians which I have specified comes nearer home and should press upon our minds and hearts more strongly. It is a practical one in every English town and every country parish, and almost everywhere throughout the world where the English language is spoken. Moreover, even the most loyal members of the Church of England, in spite of the points of principle on which they are divided from those other English Christians, resemble them more closely in many respects in their modes of thought, even on religion, than they do the members of other portions of the ancient Catholic Church from which they have become separated. And in addition to the distinctly religious reasons for considering the possibility of drawing more closely together and even ultimately uniting in one communion these different denominations of British Christians, there is a patriotic motive for doing so. Fuller religious sympathy, more cooperation, between the members of these different denominations could not fail to strengthen greatly the bonds between different classes amongst us, and to increase the coherency of the whole nation and empire.

It would be unwise, if in proposing steps towards reunion, difficulties and dangers connected with them were ignored; and I believe it to be my duty frankly to refer to some which suggest themselves to one looking from a Churchman's point of view. There are two chief barriers to the union of members of the Church of England and English Nonconformists that must be mentioned.

(1) That which I will refer to first is the connexion of the Church of England with the State.

This connexion is not, I think, such a hindrance to religious sympathy as it was, but it would be untrue to say that it is none. And there is of course the danger that if disestablishment became a political question, and especially if it involved the deflection of endowments which have long been used, and on the whole well-used, for the maintenance and furtherance of religion to secular objects, feeling between the majority of Church-men and those who in consequence of their views in the matter became opposed to them might be seriously embittered. Yet there is good ground for hoping that the question of the relations of Church and State and all matters connected therewith will in the years that are coming be faced in a calmer spirit, and with truer insight into important principles, than too often they have been in the past. It should certainly be easier for those who approach them from different sides to understand one another. Particular grievances connected with inequality of treatment by the State have been removed; while a broad principle for which Nonconformists stand in common has come to be more clearly asserted, through their attaching increasingly less significance to the grounds on which different bodies amongst them were formed, as indicated in the names by which they have been severally known, and banding themselves together as the "Free Churches." But in the Church of England also in recent years there has been a growing sense of the need of freedom. It is better realised than at one time that in no circumstances could the Church rightly be regarded as a mere department of the State, or even as the most important aspect of the life of the State. However complete the harmony between Church and State might be, the Church ought to have a corporate life of her own. She requires such independence as may enable her to be herself, to do her own work, to act according to the laws of her own being. This is necessary even that she may discharge adequately her own function in the nation.

It is not part of my duty now to inquire in what respects the Church of England lacks this freedom, or whether such readjustments in her connexion with the State can be expected as would secure it to her, implying as the making of them would that, although she does not now include among her members more than half the nation, she is still for an indefinitely long time to continue to be the official representative of religion in the nation. But I would urge that when these points are discussed the question should also be considered whether, in a nation the great majority in which profess to be Christian, the State ought not to make profession of the Christian religion, which involves its establishment in some form, and whether there are not substantial benefits especially of an educative kind to be derived therefrom for the nation at large; and if so how this can in existing circumstances be suitably done. It should be remembered that in many cases the forefathers of those who are now separated from the National Church did not hold that a connexion between Church and State under any form was wrong; but on the contrary their idea of a true and complete national life included one. I think it is well to recall the view in this matter of men of another time. It is desirable that we should make our consideration of the whole subject of Church and State as broad as we can, and that we should strive not to be carried away into accepting some solution which at the moment seems the easiest, when with a little patience some better and truer one might be found possible.

(2) The other barrier to which I have referred is the claim of the Church of England to a continuity of faith and life with the faith and life of the Church Universal from the beginning, maintained in the first place through a Ministry the members of which have in due succession received their commission by means of the Historic Episcopate, and, secondly, through the acknowledgment of certain early and widely accepted creeds. This continuity was reasserted when the Church of England started on her new career at the Reformation, though at the same time the necessity was then strongly insisted on of testing the purity and soundness of the Church's faith and forms of worship by Holy Scripture. These guarantees and means of continuity are valued in very different degrees by different sections of opinion in the Church of England, and some who attach comparatively little importance to matters of organisation would attach great importance to the formularies of belief. But there can be no doubt that any steps which appeared seriously to compromise the preservation of the great features of the Church of England in either of these respects would cause deep disturbance among her members. On the other hand, it will be readily understood by all who can appreciate the changes that in our own and recent generations have come in men's view of Nature and of Mind, and in the interpretation of historical evidence, that definitions of belief framed in the past may not in every point express accurately the beliefs of all who nevertheless with full conviction own Jesus Christ as Lord. It is obvious, I think, that, if the Christian Church is to endure, there must be on the part of her members essential loyalty to the faith out of which she sprang, and which has inspired

her throughout the ages to this day. But it is an anxious problem for the Church of England at the present time—and it is likely to become so likewise, if it is not yet, for all portions of the Church in which ancient standards of belief, or those framed in the 16th century, or later, hold an authoritative place—to decide wherein essential loyalty to "the faith once delivered" consists.

It may seem at first sight that when the Church of England has serious questions to grapple with affecting her internal unity, and especially affecting that unity in variety which to some considerable degree she represents and which is the most valuable kind of unity, attempts to join with other Christians outside her borders in considering a basis of union with them are unwise at least at the moment, as tending to increase the complexity and the difficulties of the position within, and as therefore to be deprecated in the interests of unity itself. I do not think so, but believe that assistance may thus be obtained in reaching a satisfactory settlement even of internal difficulties.

For, in the first place, there has of late been among members of the Church of England a change of temper which should be a preparation for considering her relations with those separated from her in a wiser and more liberal spirit than has before been possible. Those Churchmen who would insist most strongly on the necessity of preserving the Church's ancient order do not usually maintain the attitude to dissent of the Anglican High and Dry School, which was still common in the middle of the 19th century. The work which Nonconformist bodies have done for the spiritual and moral life of England, and the immense debt which we all owe to them on that account, are thankfully admitted. No one indeed can do otherwise than admit it thankfully who has eyes to see, and the sense of justice and generosity of mind to acknowledge what he sees. And the inference must be that, although the belief may be held as firmly as ever that the Spirit of God inspired that Order which so early took shape in the Church, and that He worked through it and continues to do so, yet that also, when men have failed rightly to use the appointed means, He has found other ways of working. This view, when it has had its due influence upon thought, can hardly fail to affect profoundly the measures proposed for healing the divisions which have arisen.

Then, again, on the other side—the side of those separated from the Church of England—there is more appreciation of the point of view of Churchmen in respect to their links with the past and their idea of Catholicity. This is due partly to a broader interest in the life of the Church in former ages and the heroic and saintly characters which they produced than since the Reformation has been common among those English Christians, who are, in a special sense, children of the Reformation; partly, perhaps, to a growing doubt, as views of Christian truth have become larger, whether after all a single doctrine or opinion, or reverence for the teaching of one man, can make a satisfactory basis for the permanent grouping of Christians. At the same time in regard to fundamental Christian belief, the meaning which the revelation of God in Christ has for them, they are and are conscious of being at one with the Church.

Striking evidence of these new tendencies of thought on both sides is to be seen in the movement originated by the Protestant Episcopal Church of the United States for a World-Conference on Faith and Order, and in the manner in which the proposal for such a Conference has been received in England, and the steps already taken in preparation for it. A body of representatives of the Church of England and of the Free Churches has been appointed, and a Committee of this body has already published suggestions for a basis of union. These have still, I understand, to come before the general body of English representatives, and it is intended (I believe) that the proposals of the Committee, after being examined and possibly amended and supplemented by the larger body, should, with any proposals that may be made from similar joint-bodies in the United States and in the British Dominions, be considered by a body of representatives from the whole of this vast area. Any conclusions which are thus reached must then lie, so to speak, before all the denominations concerned. Opportunity must be given for their being widely studied and explained and reflected upon, and if need be criticized. For the Church of Christ is, or ought to be, in a true sense a democratic society, a society in which, subject to its governing principles, the spiritual consciousness of all the faithful should make itself felt.

For the end of such a process as this we must wait a considerable time. Meanwhile there are obvious ways in which the cause of unity may be promoted; viz. through seeking for a larger amount of intercourse with the members of other denominations than our own; for more joint study of religious questions and frank interchange of views, and more cooperation in various forms of moral and social endeavour. The way would thus be, we may hope, prepared for fuller intercommunion, and it may be for corporate reunion,

UNITY BETWEEN CHRISTIAN DENOMINATIONS

II. THE CHURCH IN THE FURNACE

By the Rev. E. MILNER-WHITE, M.A., D.S.O.

AT last we have begun to see the absolute necessity of Unity in Christ, of religious reunion, for the sake of both Christianity and the world.

For several years devout Christians in England have been growing more and more uneasy about their acquiescence in religious division. The reading of the Gospels, and especially the eighteenth chapter of St John, where He prays on the threshold of His agony that His disciples may be one, even as He and the Father are one, has become nothing less than a torment to those who have any real passion for the doing of God's will, or who are humbled by the tremendous love of our Lord Jesus Christ, for each and for all. Thus far have we gone from the clear mind of Christ; thus far have we ruined His plans for the health and happiness of the world; thus far have we failed to imitate or display the love, the humility, the self-sacrifice, that walked to Calvary: He bade us be *one*, and to *love*; we, the disciples, have chosen to hate and be many.

English Christianity alone is split into hundreds of denominations. The fact is its own grim condemnation. We had lost even the sense that division mattered. It is quite ridiculous to pretend that nothing is wrong with the religious ideas or state of a race, which produces hundreds of bodies, big and small, to worship Him who only asked that His worshippers should be ONE. Denomination itself has become a word of shame which we shall not be able to use much longer. It brings up at once the thought of something partial, little, far less than the Body for which Christ died; and a host of yet more horrid pictures of old squabbles and present rivalries, of contempt and bitterness and controversy. It does not suggest one *Christian* idea at all.

These uneasy thoughts even before the war were brought home by the practical results of disunion as worked out inevitably in the colonies and mission field. The language is not too strong that labels them monstrous. Here was the flower of our Christian devotion going forth to heathen wilds, meeting by God's grace with wide success; and establishing our little local denominations firmly in the nations, tribes, and islands of Asia, Africa, and Australasia; rendering it hard for a native Christian who moves from his home to get elsewhere the accustomed ministries and means of grace vital to his young faith; planting seeds of future quarrel at the very birth of new tribes into the Prince of Peace. In the Dominions, with their thin and widely scattered populations, other phenomena, equally deplorable, are manifest—five churches in places where one suffices, appalling waste of effort and money, and even ugly competition for adherents.

In England we hardly saw these things. The population was large enough and indifferent enough to God to provide room for the activities of all. The indifference indeed

seemed to be growing. We did not stop to think whether
disgust at continuous controversy had not done much to
cause that indifference—how far our divisions simply
manufactured scepticism as to there being any religious
truth—whether the obvious lovelessness of such conditions was likely to recommend the religion of Love—
whether this disparate chaos was likely to be a field in
which the Lord, who designed and founded one brotherhood of believers, could work or give His grace to the
uttermost. No, the Christianity of our Christians has
tended to be a thin individual thing, with interests
scarcely extended beyond its own local congregation,
which is bad enough; or still worse, in our towns, content
to wander from congregation to congregation, owning no
discipline or loyalty at all.

And yet in the same breath as we say, "I believe in God,"
we also say, most of us, "I believe one Catholick and
Apostolick Church." It is a crowning mercy that we do
say it; that we do bear witness so outright to the state
of sin in which we dwell; the clause does keep the mind of
Christ and our own duty before us, of establishing as the
first, perhaps the only hope of this sin-stained, war-
stained earth, the brotherhood of believers which shall
be one.

Then came the war, and in many ways the war, which
has in every direction cleared vision, and both deepened
and simplified thought, has brought home to every
Christian both the disaster of disunion, and the imperative
need of attempting unity.

You will expect me to give some account of the reaction
of the chaplains and the Church in France to this conviction. Perhaps I should make clear my own position.

Folk probably term me an "advanced High Churchman."
I should call myself "a Catholic"—an English Catholic,
if you like—, at any rate, one who cannot fairly be accused
of ignorance of the details and depths of our divisions;
nor of underestimating their real importance.

The priests who went out as Chaplains to the Forces
had an experience somewhat similar to that of colonial
or missionary priests—they exercised their ministry
under totally new conditions, and in a new atmosphere.
So did the Roman Catholics, Nonconformists, and
Presbyterians, but of course I do not speak for them in
what follows. But all the Church of England padres—
high, low, broad—tell exactly the same tale of their
experience; between them there has been no division;
they have worked together in perfect harmony and
keenness, largely appropriating each other's methods.
In a word, they have discovered how false and artificial
is the partisan atmosphere of home religion; and when
they return, will find it hard to tolerate any continuance
of it.

The Church of England is as a matter of fact divided
roughly into three sections, by no means corresponding
to the "high, low, and broad," of the church journals.
Most Church of England men scarcely know what these
terms mean. No, it consists of a devoted inmost section,
regular churchgoers and communicants—and you will
pardon me for thinking them the best instructed, the
freest, and the sturdiest Christians in the world. They
are of course in a minority, but they are actually numerous enough to occupy the time and care of our whole
ministry, which is far below reasonable strength. Then
comes a large fringe, who come to Church occasionally,

or even regularly, in the evening; who make little or no use of the Sacraments, or of the more intimate devotions and instructions provided: they are well disposed; but are not consciously prepared to make *sacrifices* for their faith; and indeed are somewhat ignorant of its contents and demands. Then thirdly, there is a yet vaster multitude, baptised, married, and buried, perhaps by the Church, and therefore counting themselves Church of England, but who come but rarely within the orbit of Church life and teaching; and who, not to mince words, are semi-pagan. Only *semi*-pagan because the ethics, morals and traditions of England are Christian; and these people, knowing little of Jesus Christ, and understanding less, and not consciously moved by Him, yet not infrequently rise to heights of love and sacrifice which would adorn the life of a saint.

The mass of our parishioners in France, then, was not made up of the inner circle—we were lucky if we found three or four in a unit—but of the ill-instructed fringe, and the totally ignorant multitudes. The horror and boredom of war, the personal insecurity, the difficulty of understanding the ways of God, made all friendly to the parson with whom hitherto they had never come into contact; and caused large numbers to think things out, and to hunger for an understanding of God. Religion became a common topic of discussion. The padres found themselves in a larger world, where old labels and divisions simply had no meaning; and where the first necessity and work was to preach Christ and teach the meaning of the Faith. They felt also, very quickly, that this interest in ultimate things did not mean that men became friendly to organised religion in any form. On the contrary, their hostility and distrust toward all religious bodies were marked. The chaplains had that common and dreadful experience of foreign missionaries, of feeling themselves alone, closed round by thick dark walls of unsympathy and worse. They longed for the help and support of any genuine friend of Christ, whatever body he belonged to. I was called upon to preach the National Mission in a peculiarly hostile and irresponsive camp of motor lorry drivers, who much resented the use of "their" Y.M.C.A. hut for such religious purposes. A Wesleyan minister had charge of it, and got far more of their blunt language than I the visitor did; but he worked undismayed and unreservedly for all he was worth, for the National Mission and for me. The alliance was natural, real, inevitable. He and I, and some five or six men of that camp, were clearly on one side, and the rest of it on the other, of an exceeding broad gulf. With this as a daily experience, a man's values changed rapidly; and it became quite obvious that, even to begin to fight the battle of Christianity in the modern world, Christians must be united.

This assurance was reinforced by the quite extraordinary scandal that the mere fact of religious disunion caused both to officers and men. It was the big, obvious "damper" on the very threshold of Christianity—"see how these Christians hate one another." Officers would throw the taunt up again and again in the Mess, and the men lying down to talk themselves to sleep in their comfortless barns would begin to talk about religion with at heart a wistful longing to understand it and know its help and power. At once, someone would bring up the picture of squabbling denominations, and the wistfulness and hope would be slain by scorn. Next day and every day, the glaring scandal would be laid before the chaplain; who had little enough to answer. Of course, it is quite false to suppose that the existence and continuance of division are due to the clergy. Our English schisms have been caused at least as much by over-eager laymen as by over-eager clergy; and I think if it were left to the clergy alone the process of reuniting would be very rapid. In our Division, for instance, the three Nonconformist Chaplains to the Forces and I used to talk over the whole question; one was an orthodox Wesleyan, another a Primitive, and the other a United Methodist; and they did not hesitate to say that Methodist reunion had taken place more than ten years ago if it had been left to the ministers alone. But the average Englishman naturally blames the official representatives of religion, their ministries, for the obvious and open disgrace of division in the religion of love; he is ignorant of the excuses that history, and the real importance of the matters in dispute, afford; he only sees the evil fact; and it is quite enough by itself to excuse his closer association with so harsh a contradiction of the first principle of Christ and Christianity.

Then again in France, one came up violently against the sheer nuisance and waste of division. Imagine upon a Friday every C.O. and adjutant (and adjutants are always over-worked) of every unit approached by three Chaplains—Church of England, Roman Catholic, and Nonconformist; and requested to make different arrangements at different times for different fractions of his command to attend divine service on the Sunday. This in the midst of modern war, where organisation for war purposes is complex and laborious enough. The mere typing and circulating of these arrangements at Brigade and Divisional H.Q. mean in sum total a vast expenditure of paper and labour. The chaplains, who, I hope, are at least gentlomen, feel considerable shame at being the guiltless authors of these confusions. And the effect is so deplorable. Just when the nation is one, just when each military unit seeks to promote, for mere military efficiency, the *esprit de corps* of its oneness, the religion of the one Christ enters as a thing which almost flaunts fissure. Or again, think of the mere waste of pastoral efficiency involved in this fact. Each infantry brigade consists roughly of four battalions, and three or four somewhat smaller units (R.A.M.C., M.G.C., etc.). For these there are four chaplains, normally two Church of England (who have 80 per cent. of the men under their care), one Roman Catholic and one Presbyterian or Nonconformist. The two latter have to do the best they can each to get round all these scattered units to provide for small handfuls of men in each. Each of the Church of England chaplains has to arrange for a whole half brigade. How much more efficiently and thoroughly, with how much less needless labour, had the work been done, if an one Church could have set one chaplain to live each with one battalion, and be responsible as well for one smaller unit. That had made it easy for a chaplain to know his flock intimately; now it is next to impossible.

But above and beyond these misfortunes, which after all are details, must be ranked the big thoughts and truths which have swum into the sight and experience of everybody. The first is this. Granted that the Church like the world was surprised by the sudden outbreak of war, and therefore could not stop it; yet that she should have

no voice at all even to denounce the unrighteousness
and barbarities into which the world plunges deeper
every day does strike men as wrong. The Church cannot
speak because she is not one; even suppose all England
be actually one national Church, if it is only national,
it will go the way of the nation, and certainly cannot
speak to other nations. For the Church ever to acquire a
world-voice in the cause of love and right means that
reunion and our desires for it must not stop short at
home reunion. Here the witness of Roman Catholicism
to the necessity of international Christianity is vital to
the ideal of a reunited Christendom. Men, far removed
from his obedience, did look wistfully to the Pope, con-
ceding that he alone could speak such a word to the world
in the name of Christ; wide and deep has been the
disappointment that it was not spoken. Here again it is
not the Pope, nor Roman Catholicism, that is to blame,
but the whole divided state of Christendom which
paralyses the action of each communion, even the
strongest and most widespread.

I will mention only one other of these big truths—there
are many of them—that have come home to every man;
where again Christian division is the first and fatal
obstacle in the way. This time it affects all the looking
forward to the end of the war, and the new world of peace.
It is unthinkable but that the new world must be one
of brotherhood, not of enmity; of love, not of hatred.
Otherwise every drop of blood that has been shed, every
tear that has fallen, every death that has been died, will
be so much utter waste. That is the one most intolerably
dark thought in the days of darkness. There is a new
policy open to the world which it has never yet tried, to

work toward *the Dominance of Love*. Every conceivable
form of selfishness has in turn dominated the affairs of
nations and men; never yet has love been seriously
tried. But there will be no chance of International
Friendship, Brotherhood, Love, if the Church, the
fellowship of Christians, who are after all set in the world
by their own confession, to live by love, to be the exem-
plars and hot centre of love, cannot conspicuously shew
forth love. How can the nations be friends before Christians
be brothers? We have only to act according to our creed;
and our creed does not only believe in brotherhood, but
in the continual help of God Himself in our efforts to
realise it. The influence upon the world even of a persevering *attempt* to achieve a united Christendom would
surely be decisive. Therefore the reunion of Christendom
becomes now the imperious vocation of every Christian,
the one preventive of our agony and loss going to waste,
the one hope of a loveless world, the clear next objective
of the Church of the living God.

Before returning to the idea of the Dominance of Love,
and a consideration of first steps towards it, let us go
back to France, and watch the relations of the various
communions there one to another after four years of war.

It is new and rather hard to describe. The first few
months, when the Chaplains to the Forces of the various
denominations arrived with their inherited home sus-
picions one of another, presented many difficulties that
might have increased ill-feeling. An army regulation
which allows the Church of England chaplain only to
minister to Church of England men, and the Roman
Catholic to Roman Catholic men, etc., reduced the
chances of such conflict; and at the same time, the vast-

ness and urgency of the work the chaplains had to do
swallowed up all other thoughts. As a writer in *The
Church in the Furnace* said, "We have heard with
mingled irritation and amusement that good folk at
home have been exercised because an undue proportion
of men of this party or that have been sent out; the
question out here is not 'To what party does he belong?'
but 'Is he capable by character and life of influencing men
for good, and winning them for God and His Church?'"
Again, the extremely free use of the Prayer Book and of
any and every sort of devotion, at any and every hour
of day and night, has broken up all prejudiced rigidity
of use. Methods that did not help were dropped; methods
that helped men were welcome, from whatever source
they came.

So arose a great harmony, a harmony of energy and
experiment; and although in religious matters the
Roman Catholics retained their aloofness, the drawing
together of other denominations, as represented by their
clergy, has been constant and perfectly natural and
unsuspicious. United services have not been common;
each denomination has confined itself loyally to its own
men; what the statements in the Lower House of
Convocation meant to the effect that the amount of inter-
communion going on at the Front would shock members
of that house, no chaplain has any idea. But the new,
fresh, and delightful thing is, the absolute lack of feeling
between, say, the Catholic Anglican and the Congregation-
alist. There are numerous occasions on which they must
or can work together; on which they must or can do jobs
for one another; and it has been decisively proved that
the existing demarcation and rivalry in England is a

false and needless thing; and that working together can be a real, unselfconscious and wholly profitable matter. Our English airs are poisoned by past history and old social cleavage: in France, the past is forgotten, and social barriers do not exist. It is a matter of atmosphere, and there it is clear and bracing. Nobody sacrifices conviction or principle, but they love one another.

I do not say there may not be individual misunderstandings and frictions now and then, but they are miraculously few. The normal temper is shewn by the numerous meetings for conference and devotion by the various chaplains. These are more easy to effect at the bases than in the line; but they take place everywhere. Typical is the conduct of a small base on the sea, where the eight chaplains or so meet regularly for devotion, and each is entrusted with a section of the proceedings each time. For instance, the American Episcopalian takes the Thanksgiving, the Presbyterian the Confession, the Wesleyan the Intercession, each of the others has found from the same chapter of, say, St Mark's Gospel, some "seed-thought" upon which he is allowed to dilate for four minutes. There is no constraint or self-consciousness in this gathering. Each is perfectly happy, and so is the whole.

It is not surprising that out of such an atmosphere and among such practices a powerful passion for unity has arisen, based on something far stronger than sentiment, and having in it some of the fire of revelation. It has not been sought; it has come; it has grown: nobody expected it. It came, naturally and delightfully. The fifth year of war will assuredly see some definite policy or action towards greater unity proceeding from France. The quiet, unhasty, resolved manner in which the Chaplains to the Forces in France are moving is in striking contrast to the hasty proposals and hasty actions threatening on the less prepared soil at home. Indeed in this last sentence I have touched upon the two actual terrors which the Church in France feels. FIRST, that hasty and purely *sectional* action on unimaginative and traditional lines by the home-clergy will give the old party-feeling a new bitter lease of life, and by ruining unnecessarily the unity of the Church of England will destroy the hopes that are so fair of yet wider reunion. And SECOND, that the local outlook of the lay-folk—in our villages especially perhaps—and local lines of cleavage, not having been subjected to the experience and discipline of France, will have the opposite effect, prevent things moving as fast as they ought, and throw away the fairest chance of buying up opportunity that ever was given to the Church of Christ. To these opposite dangers, I shall recur.

The Dominance of Love in the world! Let us see and absorb that big vision first, and its pathetic urgency: its summons to each body of Christians, and to every individual member of Christ. Acknowledge its NECESSITY for the world, and therefore its *immediate* necessity for the Church of the God of Love.

And next, before considering practical steps, let us recall certain postulates and axioms, which in any attempt to realise so magnificent a vision must always be borne in mind, lest, in our human frailty and selfwill, we head straight for new misunderstandings and disasters[1].

---

[1] In the paragraphs which follow, I owe much to the Bishop of Zanzibar's *The Fulness of Christ*, perhaps the deepest and ablest of all the numerous Anglican books on Reunion.

1. The importance of unity is so great, and division has been found so calamitous, and the words of Christ are so definite on the subject, that I think all would admit now that *Division is only to be prolonged for causes that are backed by divine command.* The larger Christian bodies are separated by convictions of great importance; but a severe and honest self-examination will probably lessen the number of differences which can justify the responsibility of so disastrous a thing as separation, and then we can set afoot conferences to deal with what remain. Human temperament, upbringing, tradition, human haste and pride have much to do with the birth, stabilising and continuance of division. A rare self-abnegation in our ecclesiastical history was the partial suicide of the Non-juring schism, and it has never been repeated; there were many great saints among the Nonjurors. If they could not take the oath of allegiance to William III, and therefore could not remain in the Church of England, the best of them recognised that their individual difficulty would not excuse them if they perpetuated themselves as a Church. In any junction of existing divisions, differing customs and methods of worship and organisation can be and should be safeguarded. That would only make the more for the health of the one Body. But, division itself is only to be prolonged for causes that are, or seem to be by conscience, backed by divine command, and the first step in all work for reunion will be the isolating of these causes from lesser things, and their careful and prayerful reconsideration.

A grand example of such process, of course, has been the Conference of the leaders of our English denominations, at the inspiration of the American Committee of

Faith and Order, which during 1917 faced the question
of Episcopacy. The findings of its "second interim report"
are nothing less than a landmark in Church History. You
remember that roughly it was this: that any corporate
reunion can only come in the acceptance of the historical
Episcopate; but that the conception and use of Episcopacy in the Church has been a limited one: there are
many ways of regarding and using bishops besides the
monarchical or "prelatical" way exemplified by the
Church of England. This is a first proof that when truths,
keenly felt and seemingly rival, are discussed in Conference spirit, the angularities that offend disappear; and
wider, bigger truth comes into the possession of all. It
will be so more and more. By faith we can already see
that the labour of understanding unto reunion is bound
to be an immense *creative* period in the Church of God.

2. Our second axiom sounds discouraging. Just this—
that unity is, humanly speaking, impossible. Reunion
means great changes of heart in great communions of
men, and we all know how hard it is to effect change of
heart even in the individual. We must not think that no
price will have to be paid for so good a result, both by
whole communions, and by the members composing
them; and that the whole force of inherited prejudice, past
history, and present wilfulness, ignorance, and sincere
conviction will not arise in opposition. The difficulty
even of approaching Rome illustrates vividly our task.
The Unity of Christendom is a meaningless expression
without that vast international Church, without her
rich stores of devotion and experience, without her
unbending witness to the first things of faith, worship
and self-sacrifice. Here the "impossibility" is open and

honest, but I do not know that the difficulties will be greater than those, less obvious as yet, between other denominations. Yet with God all things are possible. This is only the MIRACLE which He has set the faith of modern Christians to perform.

3. Thirdly then, our rule must be, to hasten slowly. We are not dealing with matters susceptible of mere arrangement, but with *convictions*, which have deep roots in history, and cling passionately round the individual. Convictions can only be modified or changed gradually, by love and deeper spiritual learning. Bully or outrage a conviction, and you double its strength. That is why argument seldom does aught but harm. Argument is an attack upon another man's convictions, or semi-convictions, and inevitably fails to do anything but stiffen them. Inevitably therefore will hasty action by individuals or sections, for instance in the Church of England, for which other sections are not ready, throw these into suspicion and opposition. I speak of my own Communion and say deliberately, that if at the moment, either an individual, or a section—any section—of it goes galloping off, be its zeal and hope never so pure and splendid, on private roads, the whole desire for unity, and therefore the cause of unity, will be gravely damaged.

For the whole Church of England—I think that can be truly said—has now an unutterable desire for the joy of Unity; it is, further, convinced that action must be taken; but it is by no means convinced that certain actions—to take a concrete example, free interchange of pulpits with Nonconformists—are as yet either helpful or right. If one part adopt such a policy, hostilely and sectionally, it will simply throw others into convinced opposition and retard the whole desire for decades. Questions of deepest implication cannot be settled in haste. Before approaching at all, we must find the right methods of approach. Quite rightly, the American "World Conference for the consideration of questions touching Faith and Order," paid, from the start, the utmost, an uniquely scientific, attention to right method; their patience has been lightning-swift in result. It did not even go so far as to say, "We will confer, that is the right method"; it said, "We will learn how to confer." It was a new and by no means easy exercise, but it has been learned, and the English Conference mentioned above, "the landmark," arose by its inspiration and worked by its methods.

A wrong method of approach is equally well illustrated by the gathering of Evangelical clergy at Cheltenham[1] early in the Spring. They discussed to some purpose, and at the end of a few days had drawn out a series of some dozen articles of principle and action. Some were unexceptionable, others went beyond what either the Bishops or other sections of the Church are yet ready to do. Such sectional action simply heads for disaster and vexation. And it is so foolish, so great and difficult an end being in view. Why should any *sections* of the Church meet or deal at all on this matter, except to put their views humbly at the disposal of their brethren in the Church? This matter concerns the *whole* Church; any

---

[1] It is fair to state that after this lecture was delivered, I received a note from one who had been at Cheltenham, saying that my references to it gave an inaccurate impression; and that the findings were only "an expression of opinion." To those, however, who read the published account of the meeting, whether in the *Record* or *Guardian*, much more seemed to be intended.

action is futile which does not carry the whole Church with it, and the whole Church is keen and anxious enough over the problem to be able to agree upon methods and policies which combine depth, wisdom, patience, and order. We have seen how titanic the labour is; impatience will help nothing; here if anywhere is needed the love that is patient, and ready for the travail of waiting and praying.

The cry of generous souls of course is "Something must be *done.*" Of course it must; but let anybody consider what sheer miracles of changed convictions on Unity have been "done" within ten, and even five years. Better than any such immediate action which would certainly cause division, is the enlarging of the scope and sphere of this miracle, so that the friendly conditions of France are naturally reproduced in England.

With these precautions, then, let us see what can be done with universal consent.

(*a*) The first thing is to turn the intellectual opinion that Christian division is wrong, and unity necessary, into a general passion. That is to say, we want to develop among us the *motive of love.* We all talk about love glibly, and about brotherhood and a new world, with very little sense of what these terms involve in the individual life. I am sure that we hardly know yet what love means nor what it exacts, nor guess into how many provinces of ordinary life it can and ought to operate; how many heritages of past history it must be allowed to wipe out, how many preconceived notions it must dissipate; into how many social, commercial, municipal, political relations it must begin to permeate. It was for this reason that an article which I wrote when in billets near Arras for the *Church Quarterly Review* suggested a new National Mission of Love in the Church of England. For the space of a month or more the one subject dealt with by preachers and teachers throughout the Communion would be Love, in all its bearings, and with special reference to religious differences and their healing. I believe that this would be a splendid way of making the passion for new love and wider brotherhood general, an act of pure religion of highest importance both to our Christianity and national life, and sure of blessing by God. It would assure our Nonconformist brothers that we mean business, and mean it deeply. Perhaps they would follow suit in their own congregations.

It is the more important, because there is a danger of the leaders and clergy of communions rushing ahead of the rank and file. Naturally they see the vast issues most clearly; the congregation sees more easily its own needs and habits of worship, and inclines to shut out of mind the needs and interests of the Church as a whole. A National Mission of Love, dealing with all history, the larger duties of the present, and future hopes, would help to correct this, and give a single mind to the whole body.

(*b*) Then, in order that the Church of England may go forward as one whole, without the risk of sectional exasperation, it does seem to me an urgent necessity that—I do hope it is not a presumptuous suggestion— the Archbishops appoint a Council of Unity; to thrash out the whole subject, and decide on definite steps of action, both within and without the Church.

My vision sees it thus. A small Council of, say, five Bishops, and a dozen other members. These dozen to be nominated, not elected, and to consist of the leading and trusted men of each "party" with at least two of our greatest scholars. It must be small, so that it may truly "confer"—not drop into controversy—and meet regularly. It should issue definite advice and suggestion, all of which would be unanimous, upon which the whole Church could act, and act immediately. I am sure that the amount of unanimity would be surprising, and the advice bold. Perhaps the Archbishops and Bishops in accepting and issuing such reports would require them to be read in every pulpit in the land, so that the whole Communion understand what is going on, and each congregation be spurred to do its part in its own locality.

The mere appointment of such a Council would be a notable step towards unity and place the whole matter on, so to speak, a scientific footing. The Church of England would then be wisely and consistently ordered to the one end, and be thinking and acting as itself an unity; the danger of sectional action would be reduced to a minimum, and the mutual confidence of the sections be assured. Indeed it would be a hard blow to the bad party licence too common hitherto amongst us. Further, the Nonconformist communions would have a definite organ to approach on all subjects making for friendliness, cooperation, and conference, and sufficient certainty that the Church of England desired the peace of Jerusalem very earnestly indeed.

(c) There are a number of issues on which all communions could begin at once to work together. There is a real chance of abolishing war, and establishing a more or less universal peace. The idea of the League of Nations gains ground. Bishop Gore is already summoning the support and labour of the Church to it. Here serious united effort of all Christian bodies, of Europe and America, is obviously fitting and might be decisive.

There are the hundred social problems confronting us. The very working together upon these would be as valuable as the large amount of work that so easily might be done.

Education! Word of lamentable memories. The present Bill, which all Christian bodies have urged on, left in despair the vital question of religious teaching until the Churches can agree upon it among themselves. With all the lessons of the war, both to the appalling need of such teaching, and of the necessity of bigger thinking, can they not do it now? Here is a critical field for cooperation and self-suppression. Only let the younger men be put to the task. The elder will be the first to admit that long controversy and deepening opposition have unfitted them for sincere agreement. The younger men are fresh, and start with an eagerness to find the way out.

(d) Cooperation in these great matters will not only promote unity, but display already the men of Christ as one before the world. But it is not enough. How about cooperation in directly religious work and worship? "The visible unity of the Body of Christ is not adequately expressed in the cooperation for moral influence and social service, though such cooperation might with advantage be carried much further than it is at present; it could only be fully realised through community of worship, faith and order, including common participation in the Lord's Supper[1]."

[1] Quoted from the Second Interim Report of the Archbishops' Committee and the representatives of the Free Church Commissions.

Here let us once more and finally insist that the all-important thing is the development of the desire for Unity even in the most local, or uneducated, or out-of-the-way congregations. Most of the clergy now are revolutionaries for better, bigger things; but, frankly, we fear the lay people who hate change, and desire things to remain as they are—in church and out of it. That is why I should so like my imagined Council to set going my imagined National Mission of Love. But much can be done besides. Those who seek unity will be labouring fruitfully for it, if they simply devote themselves to developing social and Christian friendship between Churchmen and Nonconformists in town and village. There might well be an enormous growth of meetings, both of clergy and laity of different denominations, for conference, devotion, even retreat. We want more than one "Swanwick." Can we not go further, and draw together by experimenting with each other's devotions or organisations of proved value? For instance, I wonder if it is suggesting too much, to suggest that if Nonconformists appropriated with vigour our Christian year, they would be sharers with us of a devotional joy and help, which would certainly promote spiritual sympathy. In the same way, the Church of England has been crying out for some method of using the spiritual gifts of her laymen in church. Why not borrow notions from those who know how to do it?

These are but scrappy examples of ways by which right spirit can be developed within the single communion, or between separated bodies. The *right spirit* won, the whole battle is won.

Naturally there are many who desire already to go

much further and faster. Intercommunion, our goal, is of course impossible at this stage owing to seriously differing convictions on faith and order; and the plain fact that it would cause more cleavage than it healed. But how about interchange of pulpits? The Evangelicals at Cheltenham demanded this as a regular practice. The rest of the Church feels strongly that the time for this has not arrived yet; that haphazard invitations by individual vicars to ministers of convictions widely different are undesirable. The time has come for conference, but not yet for any facile overpassing of the facts and reasons for historical separations. Nor do we want to run the risks of indiscipline and disorderliness resulting from such individual action. The Church of England can only be of help to the cause of unity where she acts as a whole. Matters such as interchange of pulpits should be tackled by our suggested Council of Unity. A suggestion in the *Challenge* of July 19 might well be favourably considered by it. There are Nonconformists of acknowledged eminence, learning, and inspiration, from whose books the Church of England already has received much. We should all be glad to receive likewise from their lips. If a selected number were officially invited by the Church to prophesy in our midst, an immense and religiously fruitful step would have been taken, in perfect order. The plan might well be reciprocal.

The same leading article proposed that ministers of other denominations should be asked by such congregations as wished, to come and explain to them frankly their standpoints of doctrine and order. I am sure that all communions might be, and now should be, more brave in explaining themselves to each other. The gain in

preventing misunderstanding and destroying suspicion
and unfriendliness would be great, and I can see no loss
anywhere about such a proceeding.

Have you read the story of the Woolwich Crusade,
published by the S.P.C.K. (1s. 3d.)? The Crusade movement and method is a new thing. Its idea is not that of a
mission—to increase or improve the membership of a
particular denomination, but to bring God and the
meaning of Christ into the life and problems of to-day.
It is doing the same sort of work which chaplains in
France do, among the munitioners, artisans, and labour
world at home. Perhaps our Nonconformist brethren
could join us here. The difficulties would, I think, merely
be those of organisation.

Thanks to the College system, and to the Student
Christian movement, Churchmen and Nonconformists
are as friendly in this University as they are in France;
and joint devotion is usual. We have a great responsibility here amid the young and the enthusiastic, and
good feeling is both easier to achieve, and more widespread in result, at a University than anywhere else.
Well, we are awake to our chances, and will do our best.

(e) This leaves but one more subject to touch on: the
old, hard, question of Church order, and the orders of
ministry. But all looks in the best sense hopeful here,
very hopeful, since the striking report signed by the
thirteen members of the sub-committee appointed by the
Archbishops' Committee, and by representatives of the
English Free Churches' Commissions. Let me quote it.

Looking as frankly and as widely as possible at the whole
situation, we desire with a due sense of responsibility to submit
for the serious consideration of all the parts of a divided Christen-

dom what seem to us the necessary conditions of any possibility of reunion: That continuity with the historic Episcopate should be effectively preserved. That, in order that the rights and responsibilities of the whole Christian community in the government of the Church may be adequately recognised, the Episcopate should reassume a constitutional form both as regards the method of the election of the Bishop as by clergy and people, and the method of government after election....The acceptance of the fact of Episcopacy and not any theory as to its character should be all that is asked for....It would no doubt be necessary before any arrangement for corporate reunion could be made to discuss the exact functions which it may be agreed to recognise as belonging to the Episcopate, but we think this can be left to the future.

The acceptance of Episcopacy on these terms should not involve any Christian community in the necessity of disowning its past, but should enable all to maintain the continuity of their witness and influence as heirs and trustees of types of Christian thought, life, and order, not only of value to themselves, but of value to the Church as a whole....

It would be difficult to imagine a wiser, braver, or happier statement than this in the whole history of the Church. A landmark indeed! The Chaplains to the Forces in France almost shouted for joy. At one stroke, the first and greatest incompatibility of conviction has been cleared out of the way. Perhaps that is too strong—or prophetic—a way of putting it. Let us say rather, that at least the question of Episcopacy and Church order has been raised to a new plane, where all can discuss it, and think it out, not only peaceably, but with good hope of new wealth of conception and polity pouring into the old, rigid, bitter, rival views of church government. In France I corresponded with a Wesleyan chaplain on the subject of orders and ordination. He wrote a careful letter affirming the historic Nonconformist position about ministry. But, he ended, it would all be changed, if re-ordination could be presented and accepted as a great outward "Sacrament of Love" which reunited us. That is more than the Church of England has ever asked, for she regards ordination as a Sacrament of Order merely, not of Spiritual Love. But let us gladly put the higher value upon it. And the day will surely come, unless goodhearted Christians settle down to accept the intolerable burden of permanent separation in communion and worship, when this Sacrament of Love be celebrated, and the Church of England ordains the Free Church ministry, and the Free Churches commission us, to work each and all in the flocks that have been made one Fold.

UNITY BETWEEN CHRISTIAN DENOMINATIONS

III. THE PROBLEM OF THE ENGLISH FREE CHURCHES

By the Rev. W. B. SELBIE, M.A., D.D.

WHILE I think that what I say may be fairly taken to represent the general mind of these churches it must be understood that I do not in any way commit them but speak only for myself. I propose first to recall the circumstances which gave rise to these churches and the conditions which still operate in maintaining them as separate Christian bodies, and then to give some account of the various movements towards reunion in which they have taken part. The Baptists and Congregationalists you will remember arose at a time when membership in the Anglican Church was a formal and perfunctory thing. It was open to every parishioner and meant very little in the way of Christian life or witness. The first Nonconformists stood for the principle that membership in Christian churches should be confined to genuinely Christian people, and in order to secure this they formed separated churches, on the New Testament model, of those who were able to give effective witness of their Christian calling. That such churches should be self-governed followed almost as a matter of course. Their meeting in the name of

Christ secured His presence among them and the guidance of His spirit in their doings. But it is always important to remember that their essential characteristic is not either democracy in church government or dissent from the Establishment, but the positive witness to purity of membership and to the sole headship of Jesus Christ just described. The Wesleyan Church, the parent of the whole great Methodist movement, arose at the end of the 18th century from somewhat similar reasons. There was never anything schismatic in the spirit of John Wesley, but when he found that the rigour and stiffness of Anglicanism made a free spiritual witness almost impossible, he was driven, like the Nonconformists of the Elizabethan times, to set up separate churches. While it is quite true that the great principle for which English Nonconformity has stood is now almost universally accepted, and that what may be called the negative witness of the Free Churches is much less necessary than it used to be, there is still room for their positive contribution to the religious life of the country, for their witness to freedom, spirituality, and the rights of the people in the Church. For a long time, no doubt, they did rejoice in the dissidence of their dissent, and they suffered, and still suffer, to some degree, from a Pharisaic feeling of superiority to those whom they regard as bound by tradition and State rule. The great majority among them, however, have long since come to feel that they have more in common with one another and with many in the Anglican Church than they have been hitherto prepared to admit, and that existence in isolation from the rest of Christendom is neither good for them nor helpful to the cause of Christ and His Kingdom. This feeling first took definite shape about the year 1890 in connexion with what are now known as the Grindelwald Conferences. For three successive years informal parties of clergy and ministers were arranged by Sir Henry Lunn, at Grindelwald and Lucerne, with the object of getting representatives of the different churches together in order to exchange views on the subject of union, and to create an atmosphere of mutual knowledge, sympathy, and friendliness. Although no practical steps directly followed them, these conferences undoubtedly did good by removing misunderstandings and paving a way for further intercourse. To many of the Free Churchmen who attended them they seem to have suggested for the first time the evils of our unhappy divisions, and they certainly created a desire for better relations. It became obvious that one of the necessary first steps in this direction would be the setting up of a closer cooperation among the Free Churches themselves, and of breaking down the denominational isolation in which they too often lived. Further conferences were held in England at Manchester, Bradford, London and other centres, the ultimate issue of which was the foundation of the National Federation of the Evangelical Free Churches under the guidance of the Rev. Hugh Price Hughes, Dr Berry of Wolverhampton, Dr Mackennal of Bowdon, and Dr Munro Gibson of London, along with laymen like Sir Percy Bunting and Mr George Cadbury. The aim of the Federation was to bring all the evangelical Nonconformist churches into closer association in order that they might in various localities take concerted action on questions affecting their common faith and interests and the social, moral, and religious welfare of the community.

Since that time the work of the Federation has gradually covered the whole country through local councils working on a Free Church parish system, and engaging in various forms of social and evangelistic effort. The representative central council has become a powerful instrument for furthering the cause of the Free Churches and for bringing their influence to bear on social and political matters. It must be freely admitted that this council has sometimes gone further in political action than some of the churches have been altogether prepared for. From the first, so representative a Nonconformist as the late Dr Dale of Birmingham stood aloof from it, on the ground that it tended to divert the energy of the churches from the proper channels and to involve them too deeply in political controversy. In this action he was supported by many of the more conservative elements in the churches themselves, particularly as the circumstances of the time compelled the council to engage in a good deal of political agitation. In spite of this, however, there is no doubt that the Free Church Council movement as a whole has had the effect its first promoters intended and desired, and has brought all the Free Churches into much closer relations with one another, and has established them in a position of mutual understanding and sympathy. Its chief weakness has been that it has depended for support on individual churches rather than on the denominations they represented. It is the consciousness of this which has led the way to a later movement in the direction of still closer federation. The lead has been taken by the Rev. J. H. Shakespeare, who, as President of the Free Church Council in 1916, propounded an elaborate scheme for the federation of the Free Church denominations. In his first presidential address under the title "The Free Churches at the Cross-roads" he put forward an unanswerable case for the union of the whole of the Free Churches of England. He pointed to the fact that for many years past these churches have suffered a serious decline in the number of their members and of their Sunday school scholars and teachers; and he found one of the chief causes of this in their excessive denominationalism, which led to overlapping and rivalry. He pleaded that the old sectarian distinctions had now ceased to represent vital issues, and to appeal to the best elements both in the churches and in the nation outside; and he urged that the maintenance of these distinctions now tended to destroy the collective witness of the Free Churches and involved an immense waste of men, money and energy. For the sake of efficiency, as well as in order to maintain a proper Christian comity, he argued that it was absolutely necessary to put an end to this condition of things. As long as the Free Churches were thus divided, they could not expect either to do their own work well or to exercise their proper influence in the life of the nation. There is no doubt that this estimate of the situation represented a growing feeling among those who were best acquainted with the facts. But it is probable that Mr Shakespeare under-estimated the strength of the conservative spirit in many of the Free Churches. And there is no doubt that a considerable educational process will have to be gone through before his proposals take practical shape. This process, however, has already begun and has made considerable way. Mr Shakespeare's challenge led almost immediately to the formation of a large conference of representatives appointed by the Free Church Council

along with the Baptist, Congregational, Presbyterian,
Primitive Methodist, Independent Methodist, Wesleyan
Methodist, Wesleyan Reform, United Methodist, Mora-
vian, Countess of Huntingdon, and Disciples of Christ
Churches. This Conference first met at Mansfield College,
Oxford, in September, 1916, and later at the Leys School,
Cambridge, in 1917, and again in London in the early part
of this year. It appointed Committees on Faith, Constitution, Evangelization and the Ministry, all of which have
held many meetings in addition to those of the whole
Conference. The Committee on Faith was able to frame
a declaratory statement on doctrine which was afterwards
unanimously adopted as follows:

I

There is One Living and True God, Who is revealed to us as
Father, Son and Holy Spirit; Him alone we worship and adore.

II

We believe that God so loved the world as to give His Son to
be the Revealer of the Father and the Redeemer of mankind;
that the Son of God, for us men and for our salvation, became
man in Jesus Christ, Who, having lived on earth the perfect
human life, died for our sins, rose again from the dead, and now
is exalted Lord over all; and that the Holy Spirit, Who witnesses
to us of Christ, makes the salvation which is in Him to be effective
in our hearts and lives.

III

We acknowledge that all men are sinful, and unable to deliver
themselves from either the guilt or power of their sin; but we have
received and rejoice in the Gospel of the grace of the Holy God,
wherein all who truly turn from sin are freely forgiven through
faith in our Lord Jesus Christ, and are called and enabled, through
the Spirit dwelling and working within them, to live in fellowship
with God and for His service; and in this new life, which is to be
nurtured by the right use of the means of grace, we are to grow,
daily dying unto sin and living unto Him Who in His mercy has
redeemed us.

IV

We believe that the Catholic or Universal Church is the whole company of the redeemed in heaven and on earth, and we recognise as belonging to this holy fellowship all who are united to God through faith in Christ.

The Church on earth—which is One through the Apostolic Gospel and through the living union of all its true members with its one Head, even Christ, and which is Holy through the indwelling Holy Spirit Who sanctifies the Body and its members—is ordained to be the visible Body of Christ, to worship God through Him, to promote the fellowship of His people and the ends of His Kingdom, and to go into all the world and proclaim His Gospel for the salvation of men and the brotherhood of all mankind. Of this visible Church, and every branch thereof, the only Head is the Lord Jesus Christ; and in its faith, order, discipline and duty, it must be free to obey Him alone as it interprets His holy will.

V

We receive, as given by the Lord to His Church on earth, the Holy Scriptures, the Sacraments of the Gospel, and the Christian Ministry.

The Scriptures, delivered through men moved by the Holy Ghost, record and interpret the revelation of redemption, and contain the sure Word of God concerning our salvation and all things necessary thereto. Of this we are convinced by the witness of the Holy Spirit in the hearts of men to and with the Word; and this Spirit, thus speaking from the Scriptures to believers and to the Church, is the supreme Authority by which all opinions in religion are finally to be judged.

The Sacraments—Baptism and the Lord's Supper—are instituted by Christ, Who is Himself certainly and really present in His own ordinances (though not bodily in the elements thereof), and are signs and seals of His Gospel not to be separated therefrom. They confirm the promises and gifts of salvation, and, when rightly used by believers with faith and prayer, are, through the operation of the Holy Spirit, true means of grace.

The Ministry is an office within the Church—not a sacerdotal order—instituted for the preaching of the Word, the ministration of the Sacraments and the care of souls. It is a vocation from God, upon which therefore no one is qualified to enter save through the call of the Holy Spirit in the heart; and this inward call is to be authenticated by the call of the Church, which is followed by ordination to the work of the Ministry in the name of the Church. While thus maintaining the Ministry as an office, we do not limit the ministries of the New Testament to those who are thus ordained, but affirm the priesthood of all believers and the obligation resting upon them to fulfil their vocation according to the gift bestowed upon them by the Holy Spirit.

VI

We affirm the sovereign authority of our Lord Jesus Christ over every department of human life, and we hold that individuals and peoples are responsible to Him in their several spheres and are bound to render Him obedience and to seek always the further-ance of His Kingdom upon earth, not, however, in any way con-straining belief, imposing religious disabilities, or denying the rights of conscience.

VII

In the assurance, given us in the Gospel, of the love of God our Father to each of us and to all men, and in the faith that Jesus Christ, Who died, overcame death and has passed into the heavens, the first-fruits of them that sleep, we are made confident of the hope of Immortality, and trust to God our souls and the souls of the departed. We believe that the whole world must stand before the final Judgment of the Lord Jesus Christ. And, with glad and solemn hearts, we look for the consummation and bliss of the life everlasting, wherein the people of God, freed for ever from sorrow and from sin, shall serve Him and see His face in the perfected communion of all saints in the Church triumphant.

The Committee on Constitution recommended a definite union of the Free Church denominations on the basis of a federation which should express their essential unity, promote evangelization, maintain their liberties and take action where authorised in all matters affecting the interests, duties, rights, and privileges of the federating churches, and to enter into communion and united action where possible with other branches of the church of Christ throughout the world. It is proposed that the federation shall work through a council consisting of about 200 representatives of the denominations in order to carry out their will. The Committee on Evangelization and the Ministry also suggested certain practical measures necessary for cooperation in these important branches of service. The scheme has been carefully thought out and elaborated, but at the same time is not too cumbrous for action, and if it can be carried out there is no doubt that it would secure the ends aimed at. In many ways the doctrinal declaration is the most important part of it, and shews a sufficient general agreement on essentials to ensure harmonious working. The fate of it lies of course with the different denominations concerned. By this time most of them have had an opportunity of considering it and, generally speaking, it has met with a favourable reception. The Baptists, Congregationalists, and United Methodists have declared their willingness to proceed to closer union on this basis. But the Presbyterians and Wesleyan Methodists have referred it back for further consideration. Rightly and naturally both of these denominations are more concerned for the moment with measures for union within their own borders. The Presbyterians are looking to a reunion of the Established and Free Churches in Scotland, while a great scheme for the reunion of all the Methodist bodies is before the Wesleyan Conference. If this can be carried out it should not prejudice but rather be in favour of any scheme for wider Free Church Union.

Nothing that has been done so far among the Free Churches is likely in any way to hinder the fulfilment of the desire which is now widely felt on all sides for better relations with the Anglican Church. It can easily be understood from the difficulties that have already emerged in the way of closer union among the Free Churches how much more difficult is the prospect of union with Anglicanism. There is no doubt that denominational feeling is still very strong among the rank and file of the churches. In spite of the changes which have taken place in emphasis and conditions in modern church thought, each denomination realises that it stands for something positive and is anxious to give its positive witness in the best possible way. It has therefore been an essential of reunion that any scheme proposed shall not interfere with the autonomy of any individual denomination and shall allow full scope for its genius. It is equally necessary that this should be preserved in any scheme contemplated for reunion with Anglicanism. The Free Churches are not disposed to bate anything of their freedom or to sink their identity in any national church. If, however, any scheme can be devised which will preserve their individuality and give them scope for their special witness and at the same time avoid the dissensions and divisions which have so marred their relations with Anglicanism in the past it is likely to meet with a very warm welcome. The war has brought home to all thinking men in the churches the imperative need that there is for closer union and for a more united testimony. And they are conscious that if they are to face the increasing difficulties of the future all the churches must be able to stand together, to cooperate in Christian service, and to speak with one voice.

It is therefore regarded by them as a welcome sign of the times that there should be a world-wide desire for Christian reunion, and that this should have begun to take practical shape just before the outbreak of the war. The movement was initiated by the Protestant Episcopal

Church- of America supported by practically all the churches in that country. It first took shape in proposals for a world-wide conference on Faith and Order with a view of promoting the visible unity of the body of Christ. But for the war this conference would have been held already, but under existing circumstances the work has had to be confined to preparations for it on both sides of the Atlantic. In this country the work has been mainly done by a joint Conference, consisting of representatives of the Committee appointed by the Archbishops of Canterbury and York, and of commissions appointed by the various Free Churches, in order to promote the Faith and Order movement. This Conference has held repeated meetings in the historic Jerusalem Chamber at Westminster and elsewhere, and has published two interim reports "Towards Christian Unity" which are of the utmost importance. These reports represent the work of a sub-committee but have received the general sanction of the whole Conference. The first report contains the following statement of agreement on matters of faith, which is "offered not as a creed for subscription, or as committing in any way the churches thus represented, but as indicating a large measure of substantial agreement and also as affording material for further investigation and consideration":

A STATEMENT OF AGREEMENT ON MATTERS OF FAITH

We, who belong to different Christian Communions and are engaged in the discussion of questions of Faith and Order, desire to affirm our agreement upon certain foundation truths as the basis of a spiritual and rational creed and life for all mankind. We express them as follows:

(1) As Christians we believe that, while there is some knowledge of God to be found among all races of men and some measure of

divine grace and help is present to all, a unique, progressive and redemptive revelation of Himself was given by God to the Hebrew people through the agency of inspired prophets, " in many parts and in many manners," and that this revelation reaches its culmination and completeness in One Who is more than a prophet, Who is the Incarnate Son of God, our Saviour and our Lord, Jesus Christ.

(2) This distinctive revelation, accepted as the word of God, is the basis of the life of the Christian Church and is intended to be the formative influence upon the mind and character of the individual believer.

(3) This word of God is contained in the Old and New Testaments and constitutes the permanent spiritual value of the Bible.

(4) The root and centre of this revelation, as intellectually interpreted, consists in a positive and highly distinctive doctrine of God—His nature, character and will. From this doctrine of God follows a certain sequence of doctrines concerning creation, human nature and destiny, sin, individual and racial, redemption through the incarnation of the Son of God and His atoning death and resurrection, the mission and operation of the Holy Spirit, the Holy Trinity, the Church, the last things, and Christian life and duty, individual and social: all these cohere with and follow from this doctrine of God.

(5) Since Christianity offers an historical revelation of God, the coherence and sequence of Christian doctrine involve a necessary synthesis of idea and fact such as is presented to us in the New Testament and in the Apostles' and Nicene Creeds: and these Creeds both in their statements of historical fact and in their statements of doctrine affirm essential elements of the Christian faith as contained in Scripture, which the Church could never abandon without abandoning its basis in the word of God.

(6) We hold that there is no contradiction between the acceptance of the miracles recited in the Creeds and the acceptance of the principle of order in nature as assumed in scientific enquiry, and we hold equally that the acceptance of miracles is not forbidden by the historical evidence candidly and impartially investigated by critical methods.

This was followed by a statement of agreement on matters relating to order as follows:

With thankfulness to the Head of the Church for the spirit of unity He has shed abroad in our hearts we go on to express our common conviction on the following matters:

(1) That it is the purpose of our Lord that believers in Him should be, as in the beginning they were, one visible society—His body with many members—which in every age and place should maintain the communion of saints in the unity of the Spirit and should be capable of a common witness and a common activity.

(2) That our Lord ordained, in addition to the preaching of His Gospel, the Sacraments of Baptism and of the Lord's Supper, as not only declaratory symbols, but also effective channels of His grace and gifts for the salvation and sanctification of men, and that these Sacraments being essentially social ordinances were intended to affirm the obligation of corporate fellowship as well as individual confession of Him.

(3) That our Lord, in addition to the bestowal of the Holy Spirit in a variety of gifts and graces upon the whole Church, also conferred upon it by the self-same Spirit a Ministry of manifold gifts and functions, to maintain the unity and continuity of its witness and work.

In subsequent discussions a very considerable advance was made on the positions here laid down. It was felt that if ever reunion was to become a reality the question of order must be frankly faced, and the following statements were put forth for the consideration of the churches concerned, not as a final solution, but as the necessary basis for discussion in framing a practical scheme:

1. That continuity with the historic Episcopate should be effectively preserved.

2. That in order that the rights and responsibilities of the whole Christian community in the government of the Church may be adequately recognised, the Episcopate should re-assume a constitutional form, both as regards the method of the election of the bishop as by clergy and people, and the method of government after election. It is perhaps necessary that we should call to mind that such was the primitive ideal and practice of Episcopacy and it so remains in many Episcopal communions to-day.

3. That acceptance of the fact of Episcopacy and not any theory as to its character should be all that is asked for. We think that this may be the more easily taken for granted as the acceptance of any such theory is not now required of ministers of the Church

of England. It would no doubt be necessary before any arrangement for corporate reunion could be made to discuss the exact functions which it may be agreed to recognise as belonging to the Episcopate, but we think this can be left to the future.

The first point to note in regard to the work of this Conference is the remarkable unanimity achieved in regard to Christian doctrine. While there is no intention of binding any of the parties to the *ipsissima verba* of any doctrinal declaration, but rather every desire to allow for varieties of expression, it is now perfectly clear that there is among all the churches concerned a substantial agreement on the main and essential matters of the Christian faith. This supplies the most real and hopeful basis for the vital union of churches thus minded, and makes their continued separation and antagonism intolerable. The more closely this aspect of the situation is explored the more clearly does it lead to the conclusion that those who are so largely one in aim, intention, and desire should find some genuine and practical expression of their unity. The question of church order is more difficult; but here again much has happened of late to justify a reconsideration of the position on both sides. On the one hand recent investigations into early church history have shewn that no one form of church government can claim exclusive scriptural or Apostolic authority. Under the guidance of the Spirit of God the Church has in the past adapted herself and her organization to the needs of the times in order the better to do the work of the Kingdom. Men are coming now to see that the test of a true Church is not conformity to type but effectiveness in fulfilling the will of her Lord, and that therefore organization need not be of a single uniform type. So we find denominations like the Baptists and Congregationalists setting up superintendents (overseers, Bishops) over their churches because the needs of the time demand such supervision. And on the other hand we find Anglicans inclining to exchange prelacy for a more modest and elective form of episcopacy. In this respect the two extremes are drawing together to an extent which would have been incredible twenty years ago, and, given good will, it should be possible to find even here a real *modus vivendi*.

The same may be said with regard to other movements which have been recently set on foot in the direction of a better common understanding between Anglicans and Free Churchmen. It is recognised that one of the greatest obstacles is still the so-called religious education controversy. Both sides are becoming a little ashamed of their attitude to this question in the past. They realise that the true interests of education have been gravely imperilled by making it a bone of contention among the churches, and they are beginning to look at the whole matter afresh from the point of view of the good of the child rather than from that of their denominational interests. Some important conferences have been held at Lambeth in the course of which the Bishop of Oxford has put forth a scheme for relegating the conduct of religious teaching in the elementary schools to interdenominational committees elected *ad hoc*. This scheme is still under discussion and at the moment is not regarded very favourably by extremists on either side, but it is all to the good that the matter should have been raised in so friendly and conciliatory a spirit and, whenever the time is ripe, it may be hoped that the way to agreement will be more open than it has ever been yet.

Further the rise and rapid growth of the Life and Liberty movement within the Established Church is something like a portent and one that Nonconformists cannot but regard with the deepest interest and sympathy. They may perhaps be forgiven if they see in it an attempt to win from within the Church just those privileges and liberties for the sake of which their ancestors came out many years ago. With a great price they bought this freedom and they rejoice in this new movement as a real vindication of the cause for which they have so long contended and as representing a body of opinion within the establishment the existence of which, whatever may be its immediate result, is sure to make a common understanding in the future more attainable. They may have serious doubts whether the aims of the movement are ever to be obtained without the Disestablishment of the Church, but for all that they wish it well and rejoice in the spirit to which it points.

One more sign of the times may be mentioned. During the last 18 months yet another Conference has been set on foot, this time between Nonconformists and Evangelical Anglicans, and has come very near to a common understanding on such vital matters as inter-communion and interchange of pulpits. It is recognised that there can be no real Christian unity without such interchange, and the fact that a growing number of Anglican clergy are prepared to discuss the question and that there is no real difficulty on the Nonconformist side is again a ground of hope. It should be understood however that on the Nonconformist side there is no desire for

universal and indiscriminate facilities in the directions
indicated. They do not want a kind of general post
among the pulpits of the land, nor do they ask that their
people should desert their own ordinances for those of
the Established Church. Their people indeed have no
such desire. They love the simplicity and homeliness of
their own communion services and would not exchange
them if they could. But they do feel that to be debarred
from communicating when there is no church of their
own order available is a real hardship, and they know
that nothing would make for comity among the churches
so surely as an occasional interchange of pulpits. They
recognise that it would all have to be carried out in due
order and under conditions, and as long as the conditions
cast no reflexion on their orders, or on the Christian
standing of their members, they would loyally accept them.
Under exceptional circumstances and given due authori-
zation on both sides, it might be possible to do openly what
is often now done in a more or less clandestine way. There
is a growing body of opinion on both sides which would be
favourable to such a course and it is certain that more
will be heard of it after the war.

This leads up to another consideration which our
ecclesiastical authorities would do well to bear in mind.
For a long time past younger men and women in all the
churches have been accustomed to meet together in the
various Fellowships and the Student movement. They
have learnt to work and pray together, to know one
another's mind and to realise their fundamental oneness
of spirit and aim. It must be remembered that these are
the men and women in whose hands the future of the
churches, humanly speaking, lies, and they will not

tolerate an indefinite prospect of sectarian division and strife. While loyal to their own denominations they have seen a wider and more glorious vision, and they are already prepared for very definite steps in the direction of closer relations. The new and better spirit which they represent is spreading rapidly among the rank and file in the churches, and has been strongly reinforced by experiences at the front. There, under the rude stress of war, denominational exclusiveness has frankly broken down and attempts to maintain it have excited universal resentment and disgust. There is no doubt that after the war there will be a strong public opinion in favour of better relations among the churches, and no church or section of a church that clings to the old exclusiveness will be able to retain any hold upon the people. In this case at least it may be assumed that for once *vox populi* is *vox dei*.

There is indeed every reason to believe that opinion outside the churches is more ripe for action than within them. On both sides there is need for something like an educational campaign on the subject of reunion and of the duty of Christians in regard to it. Difficulties have to be faced of a very serious kind. On the Nonconformist side there are still many who feel very keenly the burden of the disabilities from which they have suffered, and to some extent still suffer. They know that in some country districts Nonconformists are subjected to petty social persecutions, and that their boys or girls who wish to become elementary school teachers are handicapped from the outset. Many of them have been brought up on bitter memories, and their inherited hostility to the State establishment of religion does not incline them to any *rapprochement* with its representatives. It is well that these facts should be faced, for they shew the need there is for the Free Churches to educate their own people.

To all this we have to add the *vis inertiae* which operates in all the churches alike. Many of them are entirely satisfied with things as they are, and are only anxious that we should let well alone. There is too among certain of the denominations a self-satisfaction amounting almost to Pharisaism. They are very busy with their own work and devoted to their denominational interests, and, so long as these can be maintained, they do not see the use of agitations for reunion. They do not believe that they have anything to gain from it and therefore they let it alone.

The same spirit shews itself too on the Anglican side and there becomes a serious obstacle to any advance. There are those who regard the Church of England, as by law established, as the only possible Church for England, and they cannot imagine why any people should want to change its present position. Dissenters they say are outsiders and schismatics, and must be left to go their own way. They should be thankful for the toleration which has been extended to them and not abuse it by asking for more. For all this kind of thing there is only one remedy, and that is a wider vision, and for this all Christians of good will should strenuously work and pray. It should surely be obvious that we can no longer treat any church or denomination as an end in itself. All alike exist for the great end of the Kingdom of God and are to be judged by their efficiency in promoting that end among men. So no system of church order can be regarded as of divine right in itself but only so far as it becomes a channel of the Spirit of God and mediates His gifts to men. All the churches as we know them to-day have grown up in controversy and represent a long process of development and adaptation. If we are to test them it should not be by the more or less artificial standards of any one age in their history, but rather by the spirit, and temper, and intentions of their Lord and Master Jesus Christ. When this is done, the differences between them fall into their proper proportions in view of the failure which is common to them all. On these terms too will the old antagonisms become a generous rivalry in good works and each church be ready to seek the welfare of others in the common interests of the Kingdom which they all serve.

So far we have dealt largely with the past and with the various movements in the direction of unity which have been set on foot. It now remains to say something of the motives which inspire and the principles which underlie them. First and foremost is the fact that it is the will of our Lord that His people should be one. This does not mean surely any mere uniformity of organization but unity of spirit, heart, and will. We seek this chiefly because it is a right thing. Anything short of it is evil. The Christian faith rests ultimately on the Fatherhood of God and the brotherhood of man, and these can only be made real when all Christians accept them and make them the ground and basis of their relations with one another. Here we need to appeal to the conscience of the churches and challenge them to put the first things first and learn in the love of the brethren the love and service of God and His Church. Then we are bound to recognise in the next place that this unity is the prime condition of successful work and witness. The tasks awaiting the churches in the immediate future are gigantic and only as they stand together and learn to speak and act as one have they any chance of accomplishing them. They have to evangelize the world, and for this they will need above all things a common faith, a common witness, and a common sacrifice. They have to leaven society with the aims and principles of Jesus Christ, to bring His spirit to bear on all social, political, commercial, and industrial undertakings, and for this too they will need the united weight of all their influence and the passion of a great common crusade. The devil is a great master of strategy and knows that if he can keep our forces divided there is nothing in them that need be feared. We must therefore close up our ranks and present a united front, not merely as a measure of self-preservation but in order to do well the work that has been committed to us. This will involve some real self-sacrifice on the part of us all, but it is the way the Master went and His followers must not shrink from it. If we but keep our eyes fixed on the great vision of the Kingdom which He opened before us, we shall not faint but go forward steadfastly and together until the kingdoms of this world have become the Kingdom of God and of His Christ.

UNITY BETWEEN CHRISTIAN
DENOMINATIONS

III. THE SCOTTISH PROBLEM

By the Very Rev. JAMES COOPER, D.D.,
Litt.D., D.C.L., V.D.

THE very appearance of this subject on the programme
of the CAMBRIDGE SUMMER MEETING, and still more the
fact that it has been entrusted to ministers of different
Christian denominations—one of them, too, from across
the Border—are signs of a remarkable change that has
come over—we may say—the *whole Christian people* of
Great Britain.

Our island was, till not so long ago, emphatically a
land of different, and diverging "churches" and "denominations," unashamed of their separation; nay, boasting
their exclusiveness, or their dissidence, commemorating
with pride their secessions and disruptions. And even
when they began to see something of the evils such tem-
pers and such acts had brought in their train—the
wastefulness of them, in regard alike to money, to
men's toil, and gifts given by God for the use of the
whole Church but confined in their exercise to some
small section;—the injury to character, the multiform
self-righteousness engendered by our schisms, the breaches
of Christian justice and charity;—the treatment of that
whole Mediaeval Period to which we owe so much, as if

it had been one dark age of heathen blindness;—and, again, the hindrances to Christian work at home and especially abroad,—when uneasiness over these results began to shew itself, the recognition of the evil expressed itself at first in ways hardly indicative of any depth of penitence, or conducive to any practical measures for the healing of the wrong. We had in one quarter "Evangelical Alliances," which put a new stigma on huge portions of the Church of God, yet left those who took part in their meetings contented in their own divisions. In other quarters—probably in both the established Churches of our island—there was a tendency (and more) to look down on Dissenters as such, to ignore even their reasonable grievances, to ask more from them than either Holy Scripture or early tradition could warrant, and to disparage unions that were possible and urgent as likely to put new difficulties in the way of that further and perfect union of all who believe in Christ which alone He has promised, and for which alone He tells us that He prays.

I should be the very last to deprecate either prayer or effort to advance this perfect end. It ought to be the ultimate aim of all of us, since it is Christ's. We must do nothing to hinder it: we must do all that may be lawful for us to promote it. But it should be pointed out to such as look exclusively towards the East and Rome, first, that a juster view of those great Churches—great gain as it is— affords little excuse for ignoring the Churches of the Reformation, and for leaving the large numbers of devout Christians in the lesser sects without either the hope or the means of supplying defects which are now, for the most part, rather inherited than chosen; second, that the divisions and "variations" among all who in East

or West, in England or in Scotland, in the 11th or the
16th century, felt themselves bound to repudiate the
Papal Supremacy, have supplied, and still supply, the
Papacy with a chief weapon against all of us alike, and in
favour of those extreme pretensions which have been a
chief cause of, and remain a chief obstacle to reunion;
and third, that nothing is more likely to bring about that
kinder attitude toward the East and us which we
desiderate on the part of Rome than a large and generous
measure here and in America of "Home Reunion"—
effected, of course (as it can only be effected), on the basis
of the Catholic Creeds, a worship in the beauty of holiness,
and the Apostolic Ministry.

Anyhow, this is what we are finding in Scotland.
Scotland, I know, is but a little bit of the world: its
largest churches small in comparison with those of
England and the United States, not to speak of the vast
communions of Rome and of the East. But the experience
even of a small part may intimate what may be looked for
in much larger sections of what after all is essentially the
same body. For the Church, the Body of Christ, in all
lands and in all ages is one in spite of its divisions.
Christ is not divided. It is "subjective unity" not "objective" which in the Church on earth is at present,
through our sins, "suspended." Well, in Scotland;
where, let me remind you, the confession of Christ alike
as "King of the Nations" and "King in Zion," and of
the visible Church as His Kingdom on earth, was never
laid aside, either in the National Church or in the churches
which separated from it (we laid aside much that we
should have done well to keep, but we stuck manfully to
this); we have had within recent times quite a number of

incorporating unions; including two of considerable
note—the union in 1847 which brought together in the
"United Presbyterian Church" the two main sections of
our 18th century "Seceders," and the union of 1900 of
the United Presbyterians with the great mass of the
"Free Church" of 1843—the union that has given us the
"United Free Church." I doubt if to either of these
unions the hope of a future Catholic Reunion contributed,
at the time, much or anything. I know there were some in
the Church of Scotland who fancied, and alleged, that the
union of 1900 was "engineered" with no friendly purpose
towards us. But what has been the outcome? Both of
these unions—partial in themselves—have tended, in
the result, very materially to de-Calvinize (if I may coin
the word) the general Presbyterianism of Scotland, and
break down narrow prejudices, to widen the outlook and
enlarge the sympathies of those who took part in them.
The second, and greater of these unions, that of 1900
(suspected then, as I have said), proved, within eight
short years, to be the very thing to pave the way for the
opening, between the Church of Scotland and the United
Free Church, of those official negotiations for an incorporating union which promise now to give us ere long a
Church of Scotland, not complete, indeed—not embracing
even all the Presbyterians of Scotland, and greatly needing
the Scottish Episcopalians—but still a Church which will
include an immense preponderance of the Scottish people;
which will be able to cover the whole country with not
inadequate organizations; which will be freer also than it
is at present to enter into further unions; which will
remain—what it has ever been—both national and
orthodox; and will continue, I believe, to go on rapidly

resuming many of those touching, reverent, and churchly usages which in the heats of the 16th and 17th centuries it unwisely threw away or, less excusably, gave up in the coldness of the 18th. We have still some beautiful old usages, as well as enviable liberties and powers. And even in the 18th century we kept the Faith against Arian and Socinian heresy: even then, our sacramental teaching could be high: even then, the doctrine and the practice alike of the Established Church and the Seceders were clear and strong on the derivation of the Ministry from Christ, and the Apostolical succession of our ministers, and yours, through presbyters.

For myself, I suggested in 1907, when it was proposed in our General Assembly to open these negotiations, that we should attempt a larger duty, and approach all the reformed Churches in Scotland. I was over-ruled. It was held wiser "in the meantime" (they gave me this much) to "confine our invitation" to the United Free Church.

The Scottish Episcopal Church appeared to be of this mind also; and those in her and among us who have long looked wistfully towards our union with her and with the Church of England are already finding that our present effort (limited as it is) is proving not an obstacle, as some of us feared, but a powerful impetus towards the larger effort. The union seems likely to clear away hindrances to an extent we never dreamed of. It is opening up the wider prospect among an increasing number not in the Church of Scotland only, but emphatically also in the United Free Church. On all hands it is "recognised" in Scotland that the official "limitation of the Union horizon is only temporary":—I quote from the *Annual Report* for this year of the Scottish Church Society:

No one is content to accept the contemplated union, should it be accomplished, as exhaustive. We all wait for a fuller manifestation of the Grace of GOD. At this season of Pentecost we dream our dreams and see our visions of that great and notable day when all who name the One Name shall be one.

The witness of the Scottish Church Society may seem to some one-sided: here is a witness from the other side, of a date more recent than last May; from a pamphlet just issued by the venerable Dr William Mair, the first and most persevering of the advocates of our present enterprise. His words impress me as very touching in their transparent honesty:

It is thirteen years (he writes) since I first spoke out in the form of a pamphlet. No man stood with me. Hard things were said of me. I believed it to be the will of the HEAD of the Church, the LORD JESUS CHRIST, that there should be union of His Church in Scotland, and primarily that its two great Churches should be one. I have never for a single moment doubted that His will would be fulfilled, or that it was the duty of these Churches to set themselves, under His guidance, with resolute purpose to work out its fulfilment.

Observe his "primarily": he quite recognises (I have his authority for saying so) the further obligation. And no wonder: he is clear as to the one great and supreme motive that should inspire all efforts for Church Reunion —faith in the Lord Jesus Christ, and the obedience of faith which the true confession of His Deity involves.

The will of the Lord in regard to the visible unity of His whole Church is plain: "Other sheep I have which are not of this fold: them also I must lead; and they shall hear My voice, and there shall be one flock, one Shepherd." No doubt there is a difference between a fold ($a\vec{v}\lambda\acute{\eta}$) and a flock ($\pi o\acute{\iota}\mu\nu\eta$), between the racial unity of the Jewish Dispensation and the Catholic and international character impressed from the beginning on the Christian

Church. But a flock is as visible as a fold is. We can see the one moving along the road under the shepherd's guidance just as distinctly as we see the other gleaming white on the hillside, or raising its turf-capped walls above the level of the moor. We can see, of course, if the walls of a fold are broken down; but we can see also whether a flock is united, whether it is moving forward as one mass, or is broken up and scattered. Such separations might be well enough if the different little companies were all going quietly on in one way; though even then their breaking up would argue on the one hand a portentous failure in that recognition of the shepherd's voice and the obedience to him which is due to his loving care, and on the other hand a strange lack of that gregariousness which is an instinct in the healthy sheep. But what if the sheep are seen running hither and thither in different directions: if they are found labouring to explain the inadvisability—nay, the impossibility—of their ever coming into line; if we see them instead crossing each other's path, starting from each other, jostling and butting one another, continually getting into situations provocative of fights and injuries?

Is this the kind of picture which the Lord Jesus has drawn of His Flock, His Church as He wishes, and intends, that it should be: is this what He promises that it shall be?

Christ made His Church one at the beginning: the rulers He set over it "were all with one accord in one place"; "the multitude of them that believed were of one heart and of one soul." And when the Gentiles had been brought in, what care did the Apostles take lest the new departure should cause a separation along a line made obsolete by the Cross of Christ; and with what adoring admiration does St Paul gaze at the delightful spectacle of Jew 'and Gentile made one new man in Christ Jesus— "where," he cries, "there cannot be Greek and Jew, circumcision and uncircumcision, barbarian, Scythian, bondman, freeman, but Christ is all, and in all."

In matters of rank and race and colour all our denominations retain this Apostolic Catholicity. How inconsistent to maintain it there, and repudiate it when we come to such differences as mostly separate us! These are differences far more of temper than of creed, or even of worship or government. We say, sometimes, that we are "one in spirit": not so; it is just in spirit that we have been divided. In creed and organisation both, and in temper as well, the Church of Apostolic times was visibly one. "See how these Christians love one another" was the comment of the heathen onlooker. This state of things continued for a long time. Gibbon enumerates the Church's "unity and discipline," which go together, as among the "secondary causes" of that wonderful spread of the Gospel in the first three centuries.

The revived, broadened, and more candid study, alike of the New Testament and of Church History throughout its entire course, is one of the ways in which the Good Shepherd has been leading us to see alike the disobedience of our divisions, and the small foundation there is for many of the points over which we have been fighting.

Happily too, we do not now need to argue in favour of visible and organic unity. "The once popular apologies for separation which asserted the sufficiency of 'spiritual' union, and the stimulating virtues of rivalry and competition, have become obsolete."

More happily still, we have learned practically to

appreciate the difference between our Saviour's gentle
I must lead (δεῖ με ἀγαγεῖν) and our forefathers' various
attempts to produce "uniformity" by driving. The
reproach of that sinful blunder is one that none of our
greater Churches—Roman, Anglican, Presbyterian, or
Puritan—can cast in another's teeth. Each of us committed it in our day of triumph. "What fruit had we
then in those things whereof we are now ashamed?" The
memory—one-sided, and carefully cultivated—of what
each suffered in its turn of adversity has hitherto been
a potent agency for keeping us apart. To-day those
memories are fading. I was much struck by a remark I
heard last spring from the Bishop of Southwark, that one
reason why we are more ready nowadays to contemplate
reunion is just that we belong to a generation to whom
those miserable doings are far-off things outside alike
our experience and our expectation.

In other ways also we discern leadings of Our Saviour
to the same end.

Through Whitefield and the Wesleys, and the Evangelical Revival, He re-awakened the peoples of England
and America to a keen sense of the need for personal
religion. Where these powerful agencies had the defects
of their qualities, in their failure to appreciate aright His
gracious ordinances of Church and Ministry and Sacrament, He rectified the balance by giving us in due course
the Oxford Movement, whose force is not "spent," but
diffused through all our "denominations." Let us be
just to the Oxford Movement: without it, humanly
speaking, we should not have been here to-day. If it
had its own narrownesses, it revived the very studies
which, while they have revealed the inadequacy of

certain of its postulates, have also brought clear into the view of all of us the Divine goal which now gleams glorious in front of us—the goal of the great Apostle—"the building up of the Body of Christ: till we all attain unto the unity of the Faith, and of the knowledge of the Son of God, unto a full-grown man, unto the measure of the stature of the fulness of Christ."

A Scotsman may be excused for referring to the debt which the leaders of the Oxford Movement—Dr Pusey in particular was always ready to admit it—owed to Sir Walter Scott, particularly in re-awakening a more sympathetic interest in the Mediaeval Church. If Sir Walter's countrymen were slower to follow him in this matter, they are doing so now in unexpected quarters. We are full to-day of the American alliance: may I remind you that Sir Walter Scott was the first British man of letters to hail the early promise of American literature by his cordial welcome to its representative, Washington Irving? Scott was a devoted subject of the British Monarchy; but he saw, and he insisted on, the duty of Great Britain to cultivate a warm friendship with the United States.

In the same direction we have been led in days more recent by the large development, in all our denominations, of two main branches of Christian work. I refer to Missionary enterprise abroad and Social service at home. Our ecclesiastical divisions are a serious handicap to both. In a matter more vital still, that of the Religious —the Christian—Education in our Schools and Colleges, our divisions have sometimes proved well-nigh fatal. The one remedy is that we make up our differences and come together.

And now this War, so dreadful in itself, is helping powerfully, and in many ways, to the same end. It is bringing us together at home, and making us acquainted with, and appreciative of, each other in a thousand forms of united service. It has spread before our eyes the magnificent and inspiring spectacles of Colonial loyalty, of one military command over the Allied Forces, of the cordial and enthusiastic support of a fully-reconciled America. Shall "the children of this world be wiser than the children of light"? Shall the Church neglect the lesson read to her by the statesmen and the warriors? Then, again, the cause for which we are in arms is—most happily—not denominational. The present War is not in the least like those hateful, if necessary, struggles which historians have entitled "The Wars of Religion": but it is, on the part of the Entente, essentially and fundamentally Christian—more profoundly so than the Crusades themselves. That is why it is bringing us so markedly together. And, if this is its effect at home and in America, much more is it producing the same result among our chaplains and our Christian workers at the Front. They are finding, on the one hand, the limitations, or faults, of every one of our stereotyped methods of work and forms of worship; they are seeing on the other hand among each other excellencies where they only saw defects. They are brought together in admiring comradeship, which resents the shackles restrictive of its play. Let me read to you a passage from a letter I received a fortnight since from an eminent Anglican chaplain now serving with our troops in France:

I see (he says) in this great war all the excrescences—the non-essentials which up till now have masqueraded and misled so many religious and non-religious men—drop off in the light of great realities; and I have seen in the eyes of all true lovers of our LORD, chaplains and laity, a wistful longing to unite, and mobilize our spiritual forces now dissipated and ineffective through disunion. What we look for more and more is a man, so filled with the SPIRIT of GOD—so free from ambition, covetousness, denominationalism, with a big heart and deep love, to make a plunge and start. We may be able to start out here, if we have the good-will of our leaders at home.

I think I may safely assure my correspondent that he has the good-will of all the living leaders of all our denominations? May I write and tell him so from this present meeting? [Yes...] I think I shall remind him further of those words of the Angel of the Lord to Gideon when he threshed his wheat in the wine-press with a vigour suggestive of his wish to have the Midianites beneath his flail—"Go in this thy might, and thou shalt save Israel" from their marauding hands.

At home, then, as well as at the Front, the will is present with us; and where there is "the will" there is pretty sure to be "the way."

"The way" (I believe for my part) is substantially that laid down by the Pan-Anglican Conference of 1866, in the "Lambeth Quadrilateral." Its four points were:

I. The Holy Scriptures.

II. The Nicene Creed.

III. The Sacraments of Baptism and the Lord's Supper ministered with the unfailing use of the Words of Institution.

IV. The Historic Episcopate.

It is fifty-two years since these terms were put forth. Have they ever been formally brought before the "denominations" for whom presumably they were intended? Were they even once commended to the nearest

of these Churches by a deputation urging their consideration? I doubt it.

Yet the first three of these four conditions are already
accepted by nearly all the English Nonconformists; and
certainly by all the Presbyterian Churches, as fully as
they are in the Church of England. The Presbyterian
Church of England has set the Nicene Creed on the fore-
front of its new Confession. Every word of the Nicene
Creed (as the late Principal Denney pointed out) is in
the Confession of Faith of all the Scottish Presbyterians.
The Church of Scotland repeats it at its solemn "Assembly
Communion" in St Giles'. Its crucial term, the Homo-
ousion, is in the Articles now sent down to Presbyteries
with the view of their transmission next May to the
United Free Church.

In regard to the Sacramental services our *Directory*
is quite express in ordering the use in Baptism and the
Eucharist of the Words of Institution. I never heard of
a case in Scotland where they were not used: we should
condemn their omission should it anywhere occur.

Undoubtedly the Fourth Article would have, till lately,
presented difficulties; but, then, those difficulties were in
great measure cleared away by the admission of the
Lambeth Conference of 1908 that in the case of proposals
for union, say of the Church of Scotland with the Anglican
Church, reaching the stage of official action, an approach
might be made along the line of the "Precedents of 1610."
I had a recent opportunity of stating, in an Address[1] I
gave at King's College, London, what these Precedents

[1] This Address, along with another delivered in St Paul's, has
been published by Mr Robert Scott, of Paternoster Row, under
the title *Reunion, a Voice from Scotland*.

of 1610 were; how they included the unanimous vote of the General Assembly of the Church of Scotland in favour of the restoration of diocesan bishops acting in conjunction with her graduated series of Church Courts; how we thereupon received from the Church of England an Episcopate which then, and ever since, she has accounted valid, though neither the Scots bishops she then consecrated, nor the clergy of Scotland as a body, were required to be re-ordained; and how the combined system thus introduced among us gave us by far the most brilliant and fruitful period in our ecclesiastical annals; and how Learning, Piety, Art and Church extension flourished among us, as they have never done since. The system would in all probability have endured to the present day but for the arbitrary interferences—often with very good intentions, and for ends in themselves desirable—of our Stuart kings. A later restoration of Episcopal Church government under Charles II lacked the ecclesiastical authority which that of 1610 possessed, and was still more hopelessly discredited by its association with the persecution of the Covenanting remnant; but even under these disadvantages it was yielding not inconsiderable benefits to the religious life of Scotland. Under it our Gaelic-speaking highlanders first received the entire Bible in their native tongue; the Episcopate was adorned by the piety of Leighton and the wisdom of Patrick Scougal; while Henry Scougal in his *Life of God in the Soul of Man* produced a religious classic of enduring value.

The reference by the Lambeth Conference of 1908 was meant as the opening of a door, and I understand there was some soreness among its supporters that more notice of it was not taken in Scotland. But it was never sent to Scotland: it was never communicated to the General Assembly. Our Scottish newspapers tell us very little of what goes on in England; and it must be admitted that too often, on both sides of the Tweed, things have appeared in the press not calculated to heal differences or make for peace. Sarcasm may be very clever: it is sometimes useful: it is rarely helpful to good feeling, or to the amendment either of him who utters it or of him against whom it is directed. The putting forth of the finger and speaking vanity are among the things which Isaiah declares they must put away who desire to be called the restorers of the breach, the repairers of paths to dwell in.

Now you have taken in England a further step. The *Second Interim Report* of the Archbishops' Sub-Committee in "Connexion with the proposed World Conference on Faith and Order" is not, I presume, a document of the "official" character of a Resolution of a Lambeth Conference. It is nevertheless a paper of enormous significance and hopefulness, not alone as attested by the signatures it bears, but also on account of the exposition which it gives of the fourth point in the Lambeth Quadrilateral—its own condition "that continuity with the Historic Episcopate should be effectively preserved."

This *Report* is, however, exclusively for England; while my concern to-day is with the kindred question of union between the Anglican Church and the Scottish Presbyterian Churches. The day I trust is not far distant when we shall see a similar document issued over signatures from both sides of the Tweed. Need I say that when this comes to be drawn up, we of the North (like Bailie Nicol Jarvie with his business correspondents in London) "will hold no communications with you but on a footing of absolute equality." In none of the branches into which it is now divided—Presbyterian or Episcopalian—does the Church of Scotland forget that it is an ancient national Church which never admitted subjection to its greater sister of the South. We may have too good "a conceit of ourselves," but we shall at least, like the worthy bailie, be true and friendly. And indeed we—or some of us—were already moving towards something of the kind. The *Second Interim Report*—it bears the title "Towards Christian Unity"—is dated, I observe, March 1918. In Scotland, so early as the 29th of January, there was held at Aberdeen (historically the most natural place for such a purpose, for it was the city of the "Aberdeen Doctors" and their eirenic efforts) a conference—modest, unofficial, tentative—yet truly representative of the Church of Scotland, of the United Free Church, and of the Scottish Episcopal Church, which drew up, and has issued, a *Memorandum*[1] suggesting a basis for reunion in Scotland, very much on the lines of the Precedents of 1610, but suggesting such arrangements during a period of transition as shall secure that respect is paid to the conscientious convictions to be found on both sides. We shall not repeat the blunders of 1637 which ruined the happy settlement of 1610.

We have in view a method which shall neither deprive Scottish Episcopal congregations of the services they love, nor attempt to force a Prayer-Book on Presbyterian congregations till they wish it for themselves. We shall do nothing either to discredit or disparage our existing Presbyterian orders; we shall be no less careful not to obtrude on the Episcopal minority the services of a

[1] Printed in *Reunion, a Voice from Scotland*, pp. 101-107.

ministry they deem defective; which shall arrange that in the course of a generation the ministry of both communions shall be acceptable to all, while in the meanwhile it will be possible for both to work together. Alike in England and in Ireland this Memorandum, where it has been seen, has been favourably received. In Scotland it —and doubtless other plans—will probably be discussed in the coming winter by many a gathering similar to that which drew it up; and thus we shall be ready, by the time our union with the United Free Church is completed, to go on together to this further task.

By that time you in England will have made some progress towards the healing of your divisions. The wider settlement of ours would be greatly facilitated by an overt encouragement from you. England is "the predominant partner" in our happily united Empire: it is the Church of England that should take the initiative in a scheme for a United Church for the United Empire. She should take that initiative in Scotland.

Could there be a more appropriate occasion for proposing conference with a view to it at Edinburgh, than the day which sees the happy accomplishment of our present Scottish effort? Might not the Church of England, the Church of Ireland, and the Scottish Episcopal Church (all of which have given tokens of a sympathetic interest in our union negotiations) unite to send deputations for the purpose to our first reunited General Assembly? Such deputations would not go away empty. And they would carry with them what would help not only the Cause of Christ throughout the ever-widening Empire He has given to our hands, but the fulfilment of His blessed will that all His people should be one. Auspice Spiritu Sancto. Amen.

UNITY BETWEEN CLASSES

I

By the Right Rev. F. T. WOODS, D.D.

INTRODUCTION

HE would be a dull man who did not respond to such a theme as the one with which I have been entrusted.

Before the war, in spite of much enlightenment of the social conscience, unity between classes was still far to seek. Indeed, the contemplation of the state of English society in those early months of 1914 was perhaps more calculated to drive the social reformer into pessimism than anything which has happened since. The rich were hunting for fresh pleasures, the poor were hunting for better conditions. The tendencies which were dragging these classes apart seemed stronger than those which were bringing them together. Then came the war, and it has done much to convert a forlorn hope into a bright prospect. This has happened not merely, or even mainly, owing to the fact that men of all classes are fighting side by side in the trenches, but rather owing to the fact that the war has cleared our minds, has exposed the real dangers of civilisation, and has placarded before the world, in terms which cannot be mistaken, the things which are most worth living for.

I propose to ask your attention to my subject under three heads. First I shall say something of the basis of class distinction, then I shall put before you some attempts which have been made at social unity, and in closing I shall try to estimate the hope of the present situation.

I

THE BASIS OF CLASS DISTINCTION

Birth and Property have been during most of human history the chief points on which class distinction has turned. Behind them both, I fear it must be confessed, there is that which lies at the root of all civilisation, namely force. I presume that the first class distinction was between the group of people who could command and the group who had to obey. The second group no doubt consisted in most cases of conquered enemies who were turned into slaves. They were outsiders, the men of a lower level.

But the master group, if I may so call it, would have its descendants, who by virtue of family relationships would seek to keep their position. This, I conclude, is the fountain head of that stream of blue blood which has played so large a part in class distinction. It is not difficult to make out a strong case for it from the point of view of human evolution. The processes of primitive warfare may have led to the survival of the fittest or the selection of the best. At a time when the sense of social responsibility was limited in the extreme, it may have been a good thing that the management of men should have rested mainly in the hands of those who by natural endowments and force of character came to the top. It is unnecessary to dwell at length on the immense influence both in our own country and elsewhere which this blood distinction of class has exercised. It is writ large in the history of the word "gentleman," both in the English word and its Latin ancestor. The Latin word "generosus," always the equivalent of "gentleman" in English-Latin documents, signifies a person of good family. It was used no doubt in this sense by the Rev. John Ball, the strike leader, as we should call him in modern terms, of the 14th century, in the lines which formed a kind of battlecry of the rebels:

> When Adam delved and Eve span,
> Who was then the gentleman?

A writer of a century later, William Harrison, says: "Gentlemen be those whom their race and blood or at least their virtues do make noble and known."

But the distinction is older than this. According to Professor Freeman it goes back well nigh to the Conquest. Not indeed the distinction of blood, for that is much older, but the formation of a separate class of gentlemen. It has been maintained however by some writers that this is rather antedating the process, and that the real distinction in English life up to the 14th century was between the nobiles, the tenants in chivalry, a very large class which included all between Earls and Franklins; and the ignobiles, i.e. the villeins, the ordinary citizens and burgesses. The widely prevalent notion that a gentleman was a person who had a right to wear coat armour is apparently of recent growth, and is possibly not unconnected with the not unnatural desire of the herald's office to magnify its work.

It is evident that noble blood in those days was no more a guarantee of good character than it is in this, for, according to one of the writers on the subject, the premier gentleman of England in the early days of the 15th century was one who had served at Agincourt, but whose subsequent exploits were not perhaps the best advertisement for gentle birth. According to the public records he was charged at the Staffordshire Assizes with house-breaking, wounding with intent to kill, and procuring the murder of one Thomas Page, who was cut to pieces while on his knees begging for his life[1].

The first gentleman, commemorated by that name on an existing monument, is John Daundelion who died in 1445.

In the 14th and 15th centuries the chief occupation of gentlemen was fighting; but later on, when law and order were more firmly established, the younger sons of good families began to enter industrial life as apprentices in the towns, and there began to grow up a new aristocracy of trade. To William Harrison, the writer to whom I have already referred, merchants are still citizens, but he adds: "They often change estate with gentlemen as gentlemen do with them by mutual conversion of the one into the other."

Since those days the name has very properly come to be connected less with blue blood than—if I may coin the phrase—with blue behaviour. In 1714, Steele lays it down in the *Tatler* that the appellation of gentleman is never to be fixed to a man's circumstances but to his behaviour in them. And in this connexion we may recall the old story of the Monarch, said by some to be James II, who replied to a lady petitioning him to make her son a gentleman: "I could make him a noble, but God Almighty could not make him a gentleman."

Before we leave the class distinctions based mainly on

[1] *Encycl. Brit.* XI. 604.

birth and blood, it is well to remark that in England they
have never counted for so much as elsewhere. It is true
of course that the nobility and gentry have been a
separate class, but they have been constantly recruited
from below. Distinction in war or capability in peace
was the qualification of scores of men upon whom the
highest social rank was bestowed in reign after reign in
our English history. Moreover, birth distinction has never
been recognised in law, in spite of the fact that the
manipulation of laws has not always been free from bias.
The well known words of Macaulay are worth quoting in
this connexion:

> There was a strong hereditary aristocracy: but it was of all
> hereditary aristocracies the least insolent and exclusive. It had
> none of the invidious character of a caste. It was constantly
> receiving members from the people, and constantly sending down
> members to mingle with the people. Any gentleman might become
> a peer, the younger son of a peer was but a gentleman. Grandsons
> of peers yielded precedence to newly made knights.

The dignity of knighthood was not beyond the reach of
any man who could by diligence and thrift realise a good
estate, or who could attract notice by his valour in battle.

> ...Good blood was indeed held in high respect: but between good
> blood and the privileges of peerage there was, most fortunately
> for our country, no necessary connection.... There was therefore
> here no line like that which in some other countries divides the
> patrician from the plebeian. The yeoman was not inclined to
> murmur at dignities to which his own children might rise. The
> grandee was not inclined to insult a class into which his own
> children must descend.... Thus our democracy was, from an early
> period, the most aristocratic, and our aristocracy the most
> democratic in the world; a peculiarity which has lasted down to
> the present day, and which has produced many important moral
> and political effects[1].

[1] Macaulay's *History of England* (Longman's, 1885), pp. 38, 39, 40.

If blood counted for much in distinctions of class, property counted for more. The original distinction between the "haves" and the "have nots" has persisted throughout history and is with us to-day.

In the ancient village, no doubt, the distinction was of the simplest. On the one hand was the man who by force or by his own energy became possessed of more cattle and more sheep than his fellows; on the other hand was the man who, in default of such property, was ready and willing to give his services to the bigger man, whether for wages, or as a condition of living in the village and sharing in the rights of the village fields and pastures. Here presumably we have the origin of that institution of Landlordism which still looms so large in our social life. In the early days it was probably more a matter of cattle than of land. The possessor of cattle in the village would hire out a certain number of them to a poorer neighbour, who would have the right to feed them on the common land. Thus, even in primitive times, a class distinction based on property began to grow up.

Early in history there was found in most villages a chief man who had the largest share of the land. Below him there would be three or four landowners of moderate importance and property. At the end of the scale were the ordinary labourers and villagers, among whom the rest of the village lands were divided as a rule on fairly equal terms.

Closely allied to this of course was the organisation of the village from the point of view of military service. Parallel to this more peaceful organisation of society was the elaborate Feudal System, by which, from the King downwards, lands were held in virtue of an obliga-

tion on the part of each class to the one above it to produce men for the wars in due proportion of numbers and
equipment.

From this point of view property in land meant also
property in men, labourers in peace and soldiers in war.

As time went on the class distinctions of birth and
property began more and more to coincide. It was
Dr Johnson who made the remark that "the English
merchant is a new species of gentleman."

The form of property which was always held to be in
closest connexion with gentle blood was land. This has
been so in a pre-eminent degree since our English Revolution at the end of the 17th century. From that time
onwards the smaller landowners, yeomen and squires
with small holdings, begin to disappear and the landed
gentry become practically supreme. Political power in a
large measure rested with them, and the result was that
numbers of men who had made money in trade were
eager to use it in the purchase of land, for this meant
the purchase of social and political influence.

It was no doubt this craze for the possession of land
which led to the process of enclosing the common lands
of the village, a process on which no true Englishman
can look back in these days without shame and sorrow.
It is no doubt arguable that from an economic point of
view the productive power of the land was increased,
that agriculture was more efficiently and scientifically
managed by the comparatively few big men than it
would have been by the many small men who were
displaced. None the less the price was too high, for it
meant a still further accentuation of class distinction.
It meant the further enrichment of the big man, and the

further impoverishment of the small man. And between the two there grew up a class of farmers, separate from the labourers, whose outlook on the whole did not make for those relations of neighbourliness and even kinship which had been among the fine characteristics of the ancient village.

Nor is this the end of the story, for the distinction between the "haves" and the "have nots" was still further accentuated, and the two classes driven still further apart, by the far-reaching Industrial Revolution of the late 18th and early 19th century.

The alienation between the farmer and the labourer was exactly paralleled by the alienation which gradually crept in between the manufacturer and the workers. The growth of the factory system was indeed so rapid that only the keenest foresight could have provided against these evils. The same may be said of the amazing development of the towns, particularly in Lancashire and the West Riding of Yorkshire, which quickly gathered round the new hives of industry. Unfortunately that foresight was lacking. On the one hand the science of town-planning had hardly been born, on the other hand a lightning accumulation of large fortunes turned the heads of the commercial magnates, dehumanised industry, and broke up the fellowship which in older and simpler days had obtained between the employer and his men.

It is a charge which we frequently bring against the enemy in these days, a charge only too well founded, that they are expert in everything except understanding human nature. The same may be said of those who were concerned in the Industrial Revolution of the 19th century. The growing wealth of the country which should have united masters and men in a truer comrade-ship, and a richer life, achieved results which were pre-cisely the opposite. It developed a greed of cash which we have not yet shaken off, and money was accumulated in the pockets of men who had had neither aptitude nor training in the art of spending it. The workers were reduced to a state not far removed from a salaried slavery, and the difference between the "haves" and the "have nots" was perhaps more acute than at any other time in our history. The causes of this were many and complex. Not the least of them was the fact that the masters of industry were captured by a false theory of economics according to which the fund which was avail-able for the remuneration of labour could not at any given time be greater or less than it was. Human agency could not increase its volume, it could only vary its distribution. And further, as every man has the right to sell his labour for what he can obtain for it, any inter-ference between the recipients was held to be unjust.

"That theory," as Mr Hammond has told us, "became supreme in economics, and the whole movement for trade-union organisation had to fight its way against this solid superstition[1]."

The doctrine of free labour achieved a wonderful popularity; but then, as the writer I have just quoted reminds us: "Free labour had not Adam Smith's mean-ing: it meant the freedom of the employer to take what labour he wanted, at the price he chose and under the conditions he thought proper[2]."

More and more therefore the employers and the workers drifted apart, and the supreme misfortune was

[1] *The Town Labourer*, p. 205.   [2] *Ibid.*, p. 212.

that the one power which might have drawn them together was itself in a state of semi-paralysis in regard to
the corporate responsibility of the community. That
power was religion. There were times, as I shall endeavour
to point out later, when Christianity was able to produce
an atmosphere of comradeship stronger than the differences of class. But to the very great loss of both country
and Church this was not one of them.

At the moment when the corporate message of the
Church was needed, it was looking the other way, and
concentrating its thought on the individual. The Reformation was in large measure a revolt from the imperial
to the personal conception of religion. I do not deny that
this revolt was necessary and beneficial. But the reaction
from the corporate aspect of Christianity went too far.
When this reaction was further reinforced by the Puritan
movement, which with all its strength and its fine austerity
fastened its attention on the minutiae of personal conduct, and left the community as such almost out of
sight, it is not surprising to find that religion at the end
of the 18th, and through a large part of the 19th century,
failed to produce just that sense of brotherhood which
would have mitigated the whole situation and prevented
much of the practical paganism which I have described.

Even the great revival connected with the name of
John Wesley brought all its fire to bear on the conversion
of the *man*, when the social unit which was most in
need of that conversion was the community. The result
of all this was that, partly owing to ignorance, partly
owing to prejudice, partly owing to the misreading of the
New Testament, the messengers of religion had no
message of corporate responsibility for nation or class.

There was no one to lift aloft the torch of human brother-hood over the dark and gloomy landscape of English life. So far from that, the people who figured large in religion were convinced quite honestly that the division of classes was a heaven sent order, with which it would be impious to interfere, and further that the main message of religion to the people at large was an authoritative injunction to good behaviour, and patient resignation to the circumstances in which Providence had placed them. The notion that the organisation of Society, particularly on its industrial side, was wholly inconsistent with the ideals of the New Testament never so much as entered their heads, and any suggestion to this effect would have been regarded not merely as revolutionary but sacrilegious.

I have ventured on this very rough description of class distinctions, before our modern days, because it is through the study of our forefathers' mistakes and a truer understanding of our forefathers' inspirations that we may hope to create a better world in the days that are coming.

II

ATTEMPTS AT SOCIAL UNITY

Let me ask your attention now to a few of the attempts which have been made to create a deeper social unity.

Some of these were naturally and inevitably developed in primitive days by the simple fact that "birds of a feather flock together."

Men engaged in pastoral pursuits gathered themselves into the tribe with its strong blood bond. The tillage of the fields led to the existence of the clan, with its family system and its elaborate organisation of the land. In the same way industrial activity produced the Guild, that is the grouping of men by crafts, a grouping which might well be revived and encouraged on a larger scale in the rearrangements of the future.

I need not remind you how large a place was occupied by the Guilds in English life. They were not Trade Unions in the modern sense, for they included both masters and men in one organisation. Nor must we attribute a modern meaning to those two phrases, masters and men, when we speak of the ancient Guild. For in a large measure every man was his own employer. He was a member of the league; he kept the rules; but he was his own master. The master did not mean the manager of the workmen, but the expert in the work. He was the master of the art in question, and though his fellows might be journeymen or apprentices, they all belonged to the same social class, and throughout the Guild there was a spirit of comradeship which was consecrated by the sanctions of religion.

For it was the Guilds which were the prime movers in organising those Miracle Plays which were the delight of the Middle Ages, and which formed the main outlet for that dramatic instinct which used to be so strong in England, and which paved the way for Shakespeare and the modern stage.

The Guild was not concerned mainly with money but with work, and still more with the skill and happiness of the worker, and its aim was to resist inequality. It was, in the pointed words of Mr Chesterton,

to ensure, not only that bricklaying should survive and succeed, but that every bricklayer should survive and succeed. It sought to rebuild the ruins of any bricklayer, and to give any faded whitewasher a new white coat. It was the whole aim of the Guilds to cobble their cobblers like their shoes and clout their clothiers with their clothes; to strengthen the weakest link, or go after the hundredth sheep; in short to keep the row of little shops unbroken like a line of battle[1].

The Guild in fact aimed at keeping each man free and happy in the possession of his little property, whereas the Trade Union aims at assembling into one company a large number of men who have little or no property at all, and who seek to redress the balance by collective action. The mediaeval Guild therefore will certainly go down to history as one of the most gallant attempts, and for the time being one of the most successful, to create a true comradeship among all who work, and to keep at a distance those mere class distinctions which, though their foundations are often so flimsy, tend to grip men as in an iron vice.

But I must not pass by another social organisation which looms very large in the old days, and which approached social unity from a side wholly different from those I have mentioned, namely from the military side: I mean the Feudal System. Here there has been much misunderstanding. Its very name seems to breathe class distinction. We have come casually and rather carelessly to identify it with the tyranny and oppression which exalted the few at the expense of the many. This point of view is however a good deal less than just. It is quite true that as worked by William the Norman and several of his successors the system became only too often an instrument of gross injustice and crass despotism; but at its best, and in its origin, it was based on the twin foundations of protection on the one hand

[1] G. K. Chesterton, *Short History of England*, p. 98.

and duty on the other. I will venture to quote a high authority in this connexion, namely Bishop Stubbs.

> The Feudal System, with all its tyranny and all its faults and shortcomings, was based on the requirements of mutual help and service, and was maintained by the obligations of honour and fealty. Regular subordination, mutual obligation, social unity, were the pillars of the fabric. The whole state was one: the king represented the unity of the nation. The great barons held their estates from him, the minor nobles of the great barons, the gentry of these vassals, the poorer freemen of the gentry, the serfs themselves were not without rights and protectors as well as duties and service. Each gradation, and every man in each, owed service, fixed definite service, to the next above him, and expected and received protection and security in return. Each was bound by fealty to his immediate superior, and the oath of the one implies the pledged honour and troth of the other[1].

This system indeed was very far from perfect, but it certainly was an attempt to bind the nation together in one social unit, to provide a measure of protection for all, and to demand duties from all. It sought to lay equal stress on rights and duties. In this respect—and I am still thinking of the system at its best—it was far ahead of modern 19th century Industrialism, a system which might be described with but little exaggeration as laying sole emphasis on rights for one class and duties for the other.

But the supreme attempt which so far has been made to promote unity between classes has approached the problem from a far loftier standpoint; not industrial, nor military, but religious. And this attempt has been on a larger scale and on firmer foundations than any of the others, for it has sought to unite men in spite of their differences. It has tried, that is, to get below the varieties

---

[1] Stubbs' *Lectures on Early English History*, pp. 18, 19.

of race or family or occupation, and create a unity which, because it transcends them all, may hope to last. As a fact this attempt has so far surpassed all others, and has met with the greatest measure of success. And lest I should be suspected of prejudice I will quote an outside witness:

A very pregnant saying of T. H. Green was that during the whole development of man the command, "Thou shalt love thy neighbour as thyself" has never varied, what has varied is the answer to the question—Who is my neighbour?......The influence upon the development of civilisation of the wider conception of duty and responsibility to one's fellow-men which was introduced into the world with the spread of Christianity can hardly be overestimated. The extended conception of the answer to the question Who is my neighbour? which has resulted from the characteristic doctrines of the Christian religion—a conception transcending all the claims of family, group, state, nation, people or race and even all the interests comprised in any existing order of society—has been the most powerful evolutionary force which has ever acted on society. It has tended gradually to break up the absolutisms inherited from an older civilization and to bring into being an entirely new type of social efficiency[1].

Or to take another witness equally unprejudiced, who puts the same truth more tersely still, the late Professor Lecky. "The brief record of those three short years," referring to Christ's life, "has done more to soften and regenerate mankind than all the disquisitions of philosophers and exhortations of moralists." For a third witness we will call Mazzini. "We owe to the Church," he declared, "the idea of the unity of the human family and of the equality and emancipation of souls." That this is amply borne out by the history of the Church in early days is not difficult to prove. The unexceptionable evidence of a Pagan writer is here very much to the point. Says Lucian of the Christians:

[1] Benjamin Kidd, *Encycl. Brit.* vol. xxv. p. 329.

"Their original lawgiver had taught them that they were all brethren, one of another...They become incredibly alert when anything...affects their common interests[1]."

In the same way the ancient Christian writer Tertullian observes with characteristic irony: "It is our care for the helpless, our practice of lovingkindness, that brands us in the eyes of many of our opponents. Only look, they say, 'look how they love one another[2]!'" It is not surprising that this was so when you look into the writings which form the New Testament. Apart from the words and example of the Founder of Christianity, few men have ever lived who were more alive to existing social distinctions, and also to the splendour of that scheme which transcends them all, than St Paul. In proof of this it is sufficient to point to that immortal treatise on social unity which is commonly called the Epistle to the Ephesians. In this the fundamental secret is seen to consist, not in a rigid system but in a transforming spirit working through a divine Society in which all worldly distinctions are of no account. Slavery, for instance, was, in his view, and was actually in process of time, to be abolished not by a stroke of the pen but by a change of ideal. Nor is the witness lacking in writings subsequent to the New Testament. To instance one of the earliest. In an official letter sent by the Roman Church to the Christians in Corinth towards the end of the first century, in a passage eulogising the latter community this suggestive sentence occurs: "You did everything without respect of persons."

[1] Lucian quoted by Harnack, *Mission and expansion of Christianity*, vol. I. p. 149.　　　　[2] *Ibid.*

Needless to say however, this point of view, this new spirit, only gradually permeated the Christian Church itself, let alone the great world outside. We are not surprised to learn that it was a point of criticism among the opponents of the religion that among its adherents were still found masters and slaves. An ancient writer in reply to critics who cry out "You too have masters and slaves. Where then is your so-called equality?" thus makes answer:

> Our sole reason for giving one another the name of brother is because we believe we are equals. For since all human objects are measured by us after the spirit and not after the body, although there is a diversity of condition among human bodies, yet slaves are not slaves to us; we deem and term them brothers after the spirit, and fellow-servants in religion[1].

Pointing in the same direction is the fact that the title "slave" never occurs on a Christian tombstone.

It is plain from this, and from similar quotations which might be multiplied, that the policy of Christianity in face of the first social problem of the day, namely slavery, was not violently to undo the existing bonds by which Society was held together, in the hope that some new machinery would at once be forthcoming—a plan which has since been adopted with dire consequences in Russia—but to evacuate the old system of the spirit which sustained it; and to replace it with a new spirit, a new outlook on life, which would slowly but inevitably lead to an entire reconstruction of the social framework.

Already too, within the Church this sense of brotherhood was making itself felt on the industrial side as well as where more directly spiritual duties were concerned.

---

[1] Lactantius quoted by Harnack, *Ibid*. p. 168.

It seems to have been recognised in the Christian Society that every brother could claim the right of being maintained if he were unable to work. Equally it was emphasised that the duty of work was paramount on all who were capable of it. "For those able to work, provide work; to those incapable of work be charitable." This aspect of the matter finds a singular emphasis in a second century document known as "The Teaching of the Twelve Apostles," in which this sense of industrial brotherhood finds very significant expression. Speaking of visitors from other Churches it is directed that "if any brother has a trade let him follow that trade and earn the bread he eats. If he has no trade, exercise your discretion in arranging for him to live among you as a Christian, but not in idleness. If he will not do this, that is to say, to undertake the work which you provide for him, he is trafficking with Christ. Beware of men like that."

On this side of its life therefore, the Church came very near to being a vast Guild where with the highest sanction rights and duties were intermingled in due proportion, and that true social unity established, which while it refuses privileges bestows protection. On these foundations the organisation was reared, which like some great Cathedral dominated that stretch of centuries usually known as the Middle Ages. We could all of us hold forth on its drawbacks and evils, yet its benefits were tremendous. For one thing it created an aristocracy wholly independent of any distinction of blood or property. Anyone might become an Archbishop if only he had the necessary gifts. Still more anyone might become a Saint. The charmed circle of the Church's nobility was constantly recruited from every class, and was therefore a standing and effectual protest against the flimsier measurements of Society and the more ephemeral gradations of rank. Obviously this process found as great a scope in England as elsewhere. It was the Church which was the most potent instrument in bringing together Norman and Saxon as well as master and slave. For, as Macaulay has said with perfect truth, it

creates an aristocracy altogether independent of race, inverts the relation between the oppressor and the oppressed, and compels the hereditary master to kneel before the spiritual tribunal of the hereditary bondman....So successfully had the Church used her formidable machinery that, before the Reformation came, she had enfranchised almost all the bondmen in the kingdom except her own, who, to do her justice, seem to have been very tenderly treated[1].

This makes it particularly deplorable that in consequence of the great reaction in religion from the corporate to the personal, to which I have alluded, the Church's power, as far as Britain was concerned, though so splendidly exercised in the preceding centuries, should have been almost non-existent just at the moment when it was most required, in the Agricultural and Industrial Revolution of comparatively modern times.

III

THE HOPE OF THE PRESENT SITUATION

I fear that a large portion of this lecture has been taken up with the past. But even so rough and brief a review as I have attempted is a necessary prelude to a just estimate, both of our present position and of our future prospects. It is often supposed, indeed, that the study of history predisposes a man's mind to a conserva-

[1] *History of England* (Longman's, 1885), vol. I. p. 25.

tive view. He studies the slow development of institutions, or the gradual influence of movements, and the trend of his thought works round to the very antipodes of anything that is revolutionary or catastrophic. But there is another side to the matter. The study of history may so expose the injustices of the past and their intrenchments that the student reaches the conclusion that nothing but an earthquake—an earthquake in men's ideas at the very least—can avail to set things right; that the best thing that could happen would be an explosion so terrible as to make it possible to break completely with the past, and start anew on firmer principles and better ways. After all, as a great Cambridge scholar once said, "History is the best cordial for drooping spirits." For if on the one hand it exposes the selfishnesses of men, on the other it displays an exhibition of those Divine-human forces of justice and sacrifice and good will which in the long run cannot be denied, and which encourage the brightest hopes for the age which is upon us.

The fact is, we are in the midst of precisely such an explosion as I have indicated. The immeasurable privilege has been given to us of being alive at a time when, most literally, an epoch is being made. Contemporary observers of events are not always the best judges of their significance, yet we shall hardly be mistaken if we assert that without doubt we stand at one of the turning points of the world's long story, that the phrase used of another epoch-making moment is true of this one, "Old things are passing away, all things are becoming new." For history is presenting us in these days with a clean slate, and to the men of this generation is given the opportunity for making a fresh start such as in the centuries gone by has often been sought, but seldom found. We are called to the serious and strenuous task of freeing our minds from old preconceptions—and the hold they have over us, even at a moment like this when the world is being shaken, is amazing—the task of reaching a new point of view from which to see our social problems, and of not being disobedient to the heavenly vision wheresoever it may lead us.

That vision is Fellowship, and it is not new. Though the war is, in the sense which I have suggested, a terrific explosion which in the midst of ruin and chaos brings with it supreme opportunities, it is equally true to say that it forms no more than a ghastly parenthesis in the process of fellowship both between nations and classes which had already begun to make great strides.

"The sense of social responsibility has been so deepened in our civilisation that it is almost impossible that one nation should attempt to conquer and subdue another after the manner of the ancient world."

These words sound rather ironical. They come from the last edition of the *Encyclopaedia Britannica*. They were written about seven years ago in perfect good faith, as a sober estimate of the forces of fellowship which could be then discerned. Save for the ideals and ambitions of the central Empires of Europe they were perfectly true. What the war has done in regard to this fellowship is to expose in their hideous nakedness the dangers which threaten it, and to which in pre-war days we were far too blind, but also to unveil that strong passion for neighbourliness which lies deep in the hearts of men, and an almost fierce determination to give it truer expression in the age which is ahead.

You will naturally ask what effect the war is likely to have on this problem of class distinction. How far will it hinder or enhance the social unity for which we seek?

We must of course beware of being unduly optimistic. The fact that millions of our men are seeing with their own eyes the results which can be achieved by naked force will not be without its effect on their attitude when they return to their homes. If force is so necessary and so successful on the field of battle why not equally so in the industrial field? If nations find it necessary to face each other with daggers drawn, it may be that classes will have to do the same.

Personally I doubt whether this argument is likely to carry much weight. It is much more likely in my view that our men will be filled with so deep a hatred of everything that even remotely savours of battle, that a great tide of reaction against mere force will set in, and a great impetus be given to those higher and more spiritual motor-powers which during the war we have put out of court.

On the other hand it is easy to cherish a rather shallow hope as to the continuation in the future of that unity of classes which obtains in the trenches. Surely, it is argued, men who have stood together at the danger point and gone over the top together at the moment of assault will never be other than brothers in the more peaceful pursuits which will follow. Yet it is not easy to foretell what will happen when the tremendous restraint of military service is withdrawn, when Britain no longer has her back to the wall, and when the overwhelming loyalty which leaps forth at the hour of crisis falls back into its normal quiescence, like the New Zealand geyser when its momentary eruption is over. Any hopefulness which we may cherish for the future must rest on firmer foundations than these.

Such a foundation, I believe, has come to light, and I must say a few words about it as I close.

Broadly speaking it is this. The war has taught us that it is possible to live a national family life, in which private interests are subordinated in the main to the service of the State; and further that this new social organisation of the nation has called forth an unprecedented capacity in tens of thousands both of men and women, not merely for self-denying service, but for the utmost heights of heroism even unto death.

Men have vaguely cherished this ideal of national life before the war, but now it has been translated into concrete fact, and the nation can never forget the deep sense of corporate efficiency, even of corporate joy, which has ensued from this obliteration of the old class distinctions, this amalgamation of all and sundry in a common service. The fact is that a new class distinction has in a measure taken the place of the old, a distinction which has nothing to do with blood or with money, but solely with service. The nation is graded, not in degrees of social importance but in degrees of capacity for service. The only superiority is one of sacrifice. And each grade takes its hat off to the other on the equal standing ground of an all pervading patriotism. The only social competition is not in getting but in giving. National advantage takes the place of personal profit, and there is a sense of neighbourliness such as Britain has not experienced for many a long day, possibly for many a long century.

The supreme problem before us, I take it, is how to conserve this relationship and carry it over from the day of war to the day of peace. To do it will call for just that same spirit of sacrifice and service which is its own most predominant characteristic.

For one thing we must be quite definitely prepared in every section of society for a new way of life. From the economic point of view this will mean that the rich will be less rich, and the poor will be enabled to lead a larger life. Already the wealthy classes have been learning to live a simple life, and to substitute the service of the country for their own personal enjoyment. A serious call will come to them to continue in that state of life when the war is over. In some degree at least the pressure of the financial burden which the nation will have to bear will compel them to do so.

To the workers too in the same way the call will come to a new and more worthy way of life. I am thinking now of the workers at home who have been earning unprecedented wages, and thereby in many cases are already assaying a larger life. They will be reluctant to give this up, but only a gradual redistribution of wealth can make it permanent. It is not of course merely or mainly a matter of wages. The only real enlargement of life is spiritual. It is an affair of the mind and the soul.

The more we bring a true education within reach of the workers the more will there arise that sense of real kinship which only equality of education can adequately guarantee.

And speaking at Cambridge one cannot refrain from remarking that the University itself will have to submit to a considerable re-adjustment of its life if it is to be a

pioneer in this intellectual comradeship of which I speak.
A University may be a nursery of class distinction. In
some measure it certainly has been so in the past. The
opportunity is now before it to lead the way in establishing the only kind of equality which is really worth
having.

Then too there are obvious steps which can be taken
without delay in a new organisation of industry.

I am not one of those who think that the industrial
problem can be solved in five minutes or even in five
years. None the less it should not be impossible in wise
ways to give the workers a true share of responsibility,
particularly in matters which concern the conditions of
their work and the remuneration of their labour.

If the sense of being driven by a taskmaster, whether
it be the foreman of the shop, or the manager of the
works, could give place to a truer co-operation in the
management, and a larger measure of responsibility for
the worker, we should be well on the road to eliminating
one of the most persistent causes of just that kind of
class distinction which we want to abolish. The more
men work together in a real comradeship, the more mere
social distinctions fade into the background. Is this not
written on every page of the chronicles of this war?

But the supreme factor in the situation, without which
no mere adjustment of organisation will prevail, is that
new outlook on life which can only be described as a
subordination of private advantage to the service of the
country.

It is this alone which can really abolish the almost
eternal class distinctions which we have traced throughout
our survey, the distinction between the "haves" and the

"have nots." For, as this spirit grows, the "have nots" tend to disappear, and the "haves" look upon what they have not as a selfish possession for their own enjoyment, but as a means of service for the common weal. Property, that which is most proper to a man, is seen to be precisely that contribution which he is capable of making to the welfare of his fellows.

The crux, the very core of the whole problem, is to find some means by which this new outlook can be produced, and a new motive by which men can be constrained to turn the vision into fact.

Here will come in that power which, as I pointed out, has sometimes been so potent and sometimes so impotent, but which, if it is allowed its proper scope, can never fail. I mean of course religion.

If men can be brought to see that this new outlook with its corresponding re-adjustment of social life is not merely a project of reformers but the plan of the Most High God, the deliberate intention of the supreme Spirit-force of the universe, the Scheme that was taught by the Prince of men, then indeed we may hope that the class distinction of which He spoke will at la t be adopted: "Whosoever will be great among you, shall be your minister: and whosoever of you will be the chiefest, shall be servant of all. For even the Son of Man came not to be ministered unto, but to minister, and to give his life a ransom for many[1]."

[1] St Mark x. 43–45.

UNITY BETWEEN CLASSES

II

By the Right Hon. J. R. CLYNES, M.P.

I HAVE not the advantage of knowing anything of the treatment of any part of this subject by any preceding speaker. I myself intend to deal with it from the industrial and social standpoint, for I think if we are to seek unity amongst classes it is most important in the national interest that unity should first be sought and secured in the industries of the country. That there is disunity is suggested and admitted in the terms of the subject. This disunity has grown out of conditions which range over a few generations. I believe that these conditions grew largely out of our ignoring the human side of industry and the general life conditions of the masses of our workers. Our economic doctrine ignored the human factor, and measured what was termed national progress in terms merely of material wealth without due regard to who owned the wealth, made mainly by the energy of the industrial population. Religious doctrines and religious institutions were not the cause of that unhappy situation, but they had suffered from it, until now we find a very considerable number of the population engaged in a struggle for life, in a struggle for the material means of existence, handicapped by belief that their own unaided effort alone can assist them, that they must not look for

8—2

help to any other class, or to any other quarter. Moral precepts have not the influence which they ought to have upon our industrial relations. Workers are thrown back upon their own resources; and in the use of those resources, during the past fifteen years particularly, much has been revealed to us of what is now in the working class mind. I am not suggesting that to seek a settlement of conditions of disunity, or the trouble arising from those conditions, you must coddle the working classes, praise them and pay them highly, and try to keep them contented with conditions which in themselves cannot be defended. I do not mean that at all. What I mean is that if unity between classes in industrial and economic life is to be sought and secured, it can be got only at a price, paid in a two-fold form; that of giving a larger yield of the wealth of the nation to those who mainly by their energies make that wealth, and of placing the producing classes upon a level where they will receive a higher measure of respect, of thanks, and regard than they previously have received from the nation as a whole. I was asked among others some twelve months ago to share in the investigations then made by representatives of the Government to discover the immediate cause of the very serious unrest then displayed in the country, and we went for a period of many weeks into the main centres of the kingdom and brought a varied collection of witnesses before us in order that the most reliable evidence should be obtained, and one who favoured us with his views was the Rev. Canon Green, whom I am going to quote because of his great experience among the working class populations in various circumstances and over many years in Manchester and elsewhere. This is what Canon Green writes:

They (the working classes) do not see why their hours should be so long, and their wages so small, their lives so dull and colourless, and their opportunities of reasonable rest and recreation so few. Can we wonder that with growing education and intelligence the workers of England are beginning to contrast their lot with that of the rich and to ask whether so great inequalities are necessary?

There I believe you have put in the plainest and gentlest terms the working of the working class mind as it is to-day. The country has given them more opportunities of education. When they were less educated, or, if I may say so, more ignorant than they are now, they were naturally more submissive and content with conditions the cause of which they so little understood. You cannot send the children of the poor to school, and improve your State agencies for education, and increase the millions annually which the country is ready to spend in teaching the masses of the people more than they knew before, and expect those masses to remain content with the economic and social conditions which even disturbed their more ignorant fathers. In short, the more you educate and train the working classes, the more naturally you bring them to the point of revolt against conditions which are inhuman or unfair, or which cannot be brought to square with the higher standard of education which they may receive. I am sure when the community come to understand that it is a natural and even a proper sense of revolt on the part of the masses of the people they will not regret their education. Out of all this feeling of discontent in the minds of the industrial population there has in the last thirty odd years grown very strong organisation. The Trade Union movement, which I mention first as a very great factor in all these matters, is a most powerful and important factor, and the country will have to pay greater regard to the steps which Trade Unionism may take than the country has been disposed previously to do. The Trade Union movement was stimulated and developed by the conditions which it was brought into being to remedy. The Trade Union was not the growth of mere agitation. The average Briton must be convinced that there is something really wrong before he will try to remedy it at all, and you cannot by lectures, and by telling the people that they have been and are being oppressed, stir the people of this country to any resistance. Particularly you cannot get them to pay a contribution for it. It was because of the experience of the mass of the workers, their low wages and long hours and the bad conditions of employment, that they organised and used the might that comes from numbers, and paid contributions which in the sum total now amount to many millions of pounds in the way of reserve funds. No apology was needed for the working classes and no defence is required for this step taken by the workers to unite themselves in Trade Unions, and thereby secure by the unity of numbers the power which, acting singly, it was impossible for them to exercise. This Trade Union movement is quite alive to the division which exists among our classes, and I am going to suggest that the movement might be used, might be properly employed, in obtaining that unity of classes which we are here to consider.

Well, then, we may, whilst not overlooking other helpful activities of a large number of people in this country, seek this unity among three main divisions of our people, viz. (a) in industries, (b) in agriculture, and

(c) in businesses. Given unity of interest and oneness of purpose and aim in those three broad divisions of the nation, the rest must be attracted and brought into harmony by mere force of example, if nothing else, with the unity which might be secured in the three broad divisions to which I have referred. One of the hopeful things, the significant things, recently uttered in other quarters from which I am going to quote, is clearly seeking this tendency to unity instead of the different interests and classes being driven by the waste and folly of the disuniting lines upon which so far we have persisted. I observe that only a few days ago Lord Selborne, who is one of our principal mouthpieces on agricultural matters, presided at a new body called into existence within the past few weeks and to be known as the National Agricultural Council. Now, that is not a body which will consist of landowners, or of farmers, or of farm workers; it is a body to consist of all three. The landowners, the farmers, and the agricultural workers have come to recognise that they all have something in common touching agriculture, touching the trade or industry in which they are brought into close touch day by day. I know as a matter of fact that only a very few years ago the Farmers' Union would not tolerate the idea of the farm workers having a union, and the land workers looked with real dread upon the farmers having a union, and now all three have come to the stage when they agree to join in one Council, and, though it was admitted that the interests of those three classes were primarily in conflict, it was recognised that by holding meetings, by the representatives of all these quite distinct interests frequently coming together, much good might be done. For what? As they say, for agriculture. So, though none of them will forfeit any rightful interest anyone of them may have in the pursuit of a special claim, they will all recognise a higher sense of duty, and feel there is an obligation upon them to make agriculture in this country a greater thing not only for themselves as the three partners, but for the mass of the community at large. And if it is necessary to do that in the farmers' interest or the landowners' interest, it was at least as necessary. to do it in the interest of the agricultural worker, and I put his claim first, not because he is the sole contributor to any yield that may come from the land, but because he is the most numerous body, and numbers in this as in other respects may well be the determining factor; and because if he withholds his labour there will be none of the fruit of the soil for which we look year after year. I follow up this statement by an authoritative one from another quarter. Lord Lee, who as we know was the Director of the Food Production Department at the Board of Agriculture, spoke some time ago on this aspect of the case, and said: "Take the agricultural labourer for example. Does anyone suppose, or suggest, that he should return from the trenches—where he has distinguished himself in a way unsurpassed by any other class in the community—to the old miserable conditions under which, in most parts of the country, he was under-paid, wretchedly housed, and denied almost any pleasure in life, except such as the public house could offer him? Those conditions were a disgrace to the country, and I shall never be content until they are swept away for ever. I do not say this only in the interest of the man himself; it is necessary these conditions should go, in the best interests not merely of the labourer but of the farmer and of agriculture." So it may be that unity and oneness of purpose and of action will be driven upon us as one of the bye-products of war conditions. For your simple plain agricultural worker will come back feeling that as he has fought for the liberties of his country he will be entitled to enjoy a little more of it than ever before, that if the land is to be freed from designs of the tyrant abroad it must be freed also from any wrong at home, and that he must have a larger share in the fruits of his labour than he has enjoyed before. My own view is that you will not on that account make the farm worker a less efficient harvestman, but you will make him a happier father, you will be making him a more contented citizen, and may make him a more profitable worker than he has ever been.

Various remedies have been tried or thought of to give effect to what are our common aspirations. One I have seen referred to frequently is one I would like to see always avoided. It is the remedy of placing before workmen as a necessity a greatly increased output from their manual labour in the future; not that I am opposed to an increased output, but I am not going to demand it as part of the bargain which should itself be arranged and carried out, even if it did not necessarily secure for us any greater sum total of wealth than we now enjoy; for poor as we may have accounted ourselves we have seen in the past few years how vastly we can spend and lend in support of any high purpose to which the country may devote itself. Poverty can never again be claimed by the nation as a whole whenever there is a proper and reasonable demand for any social change or reform which may be necessary and proper. Men are asking for a greater yield, for a greater output, for building up our wealth higher than ever before, so as to repair the ravages of the war, if for no other purpose. With all those objects I agree, but we must not make them as terms to the worker in exchange for those conditions of unity which we are asking our workers to arrange with us. Greater output, increased efficiency, a bigger and better return of wealth from industrial and agricultural energy, can well come out of a better working system, a better re-arrangement of combined effort, a more extensive use of machinery, a more satisfactory sub-division of labour, a wider employment of the personal experience and technical skill of our industrial classes, a higher state of administrative efficiency and management in the workshops, the creation of a better and more humane atmosphere in the workshops. Out of all of these things a greater yield of wealth could be produced, and it is along those lines we must go in order not merely to convert but to convince the workman that he is not being used as a mere tool for some ulterior end for the benefit of some smaller class in the country. It has been said by some that Trade Union restrictions and limitations must go. I candidly admit there have been Trade Union regulations and conditions which perhaps have stood in the way of some increased output, but I am not here to apologise for Trade Union rules. Every class has its regulations and rules. The more powerful and the more wealthy the class the more rigid and stringent those rules have been. However, the class which was most in need of regulations and rules, the working class, was the first to set the example of setting them aside as a general war measure when the country called upon the workers to take action of that kind during 1915. We must, therefore, keep in mind the fact that workmen are naturally suspicious. That suspicion is the growth of the workshop system, into which I have not now the time to go, and we must avoid causing the workman to suspect that our unity, the unity we are seeking among classes, is a mere device for getting him to work harder and produce greater wealth and perhaps labour even longer hours than ever.

The first great step towards this unity is to secure the good will of the Trade Unions. Having secured that, the next thing is to proceed upon lines which will bring at once home to the individual workman in the workshop some sense of responsibility with regard to the response which he must make to the appeal which we put before him. In short, better relations must precede any first step that could effectively be taken to secure this greater unity, and better relations are impossible in industry until we have given the individual workman a greater sense of responsibility of what he is in the workshop for. Let me briefly outline how that might be secured. It was put, I think, quite eloquently if simply in an address to the Trade Union Congress a short time ago by the President of the Congress, who said that the workman wanted a voice in the daily management of the employment in which he spends his working life, in the atmosphere and in the conditions under which he has to work, in the hours of beginning and ending work, in the conditions of remuneration, and even in the manners and practices of the foremen with whom he had to be in contact. "In all these matters," said the President, "workmen have a right to a voice—even to an equal voice—with the management itself." I know that is a big, and to some an extravagant claim to make, but to set it aside or ignore it is to provoke and invite further trouble. Industry can no longer be run for the profit which it produces, or even because of the wealth which collective energy can make. That, indeed, was the mistake out of which, as I said at the beginning, this disunion, and this suspicion, and this selfishness, have grown. We have had greatly to modify our doctrines of political economy during the course of the war, and all the things which many teachers told us never could be done have come as natural to us under war conditions which we could not resist, and of which we were the creatures. Where now is the law of supply and demand? Indeed, if the law of supply and demand were operating at this moment, there are few workmen in the country who would not be receiving many, many pounds more a week than they are. The workman is not paid to-day according to the demand for his labour. A very much higher obligation decides for him what his remuneration is to be. I have in mind, of course, the fact that a considerable number of workers, who are employed upon munition services and so on, are enjoying very high wages, but that is not at all true of the masses of the industrial population, and we ought not to be deceived by these rare instances which are quoted of men coming out of the workshop with £20 or £30. Speaking of the industrial population in the main, what was the outstanding economic doctrine?—the doctrine that the demand for labour and the volume for supplying that demand determined the remuneration. That doctrine has had to go by the board like so many other things that could not exist under war pressure.

Then, how are we to give effect to this general work-shop aspiration for bringing the workman into closer unity with the conditions which determine that part of his life which is the bread-winning part, for which he has to turn out in the morning early and often return home late in the evening? There was established some time ago what can be described as a quite responsible com-mittee to report upon how better relations not only between employers and employed through their associa-tions, but in regard to employers and employed in the workshops, might be established. That committee issued the report commonly known to us now as the Whitley Report, of which I am quite sure more will be heard in a few years. The men who had to frame that report were drawn from the two extremes of the employers and trade unions. We had men with very advanced views, like Mr Smillie, on the one hand, and we had quite powerful employers of labour, like Sir Gilbert Claughton and Sir William Carter, on the other. I had the privilege of sitting on that committee, and for some months we laboured to frame some definite terms which might be accepted by those who were concerned in our recom-mendations. I very often hear the suggestion that people will have little of it because it is not ideal, not grand or great enough, but we have to come down to the earth upon these matters, and we have to recommend only what we feel is likely to be accepted lest our labour should be wasted. We must avoid, therefore, throwing our aims too high, and we must suggest only what prac-tical business men and workmen are likely seriously to consider. Having decided to reach that conclusion, and feeling the sense of responsibility which, opposed as so many of us were to each other, drove us to reach a conclusion, we expressed ourselves in these terms: "We are convinced that a permanent improvement in the relations between employers and employed must be founded upon something other than a cash basis. What is wanted is that the workpeople should have a greater opportunity of participating in the discussion upon an adjustment of those parts of industry by which they are most affected. For securing improvement in the relations between employers and employed, it is essential that any proposals put forward should offer to workpeople the means of attaining improved conditions of employment and a higher standard of comfort generally, and involve the enlistment of their active and continuous co-operation in the promotion of industry." Previously, the view was that the workman had nothing whatever to do with this phase of the management of business, and that is a phrase still very much used. We make no claim in this report that workmen should have the right to interfere in the higher realms of business management, in, say, finance, in the general higher details of organisation, in the extension of works, in all those more important and urgent matters which must come before the board of managers or the manager himself. These are things which belong properly and exclusively to those who have the responsibility of managing our great industries, but in all the other things affecting the conditions of the workman, the manner in which he is to be treated, hours, wages, conditions of employment, relations between section and section, and working division and working division, all those things which were regarded previously as the private monopoly of the foreman or manager must in future become the common concern of the workmen collectively, and they must have some voice in how these things are to be settled. The country and its industries, of course, may refuse to hear that voice, but really we have to choose between reconciling workmen to a given system of industry or finding workmen in perpetual revolt against their conditions. And it will pay the country to concede a great deal, not only for peace in the workshop but for a higher standard of peace generally in the whole community. The appeal that must be made to the workman must be followed up by asking him to receive it in a very different spirit from the spirit sometimes shewn in certain workshops. I am not here by any means to pour praise altogether upon the working classes, and I am conscious of the mistakes and wrongs which have sometimes been done in their names, and I am therefore anxious that the spirit of the workshop should be so tempered and altered as to be fit to receive and make the best use of the approaches which are to be made to it to participate in workshop management upon the lines which I have indicated.

So this appeal which has been made by the Whitley committee, and which has been followed up by some other departments of government, is put as an appeal to the common-sense and reason of the men in the workshop, and does not rest upon any of the many agencies which have been employed previously in the pursuit of definite trade union ends. This spirit can be fostered only when the masses of workmen are reached by the consciousness that they themselves are being called upon to share in the undertakings of which they are so important a part. The importance of workmen has been revealed in a most startling way during the period of the war, and the war has shewn in many trades that recurring differences between capital and labour can be adjusted without strikes and without lock-outs if methods are provided in the workshop which are acceptable to both sides, and are made to operate fairly and satisfactorily between the different interests. Think how important the workman has become because of the war. Consider how much the workman is now pressed and drawn into all manner of services which previously he could either remain in or leave at his will. The war has made such a demand upon national industrial energy that there is no service now for which there is not a demand. Indeed, you have seen the effect in that services in the workshop include men who previously would have been ashamed to have had it known that they had ever soiled their hands at any toil at all, but who have been glad to get a place in the workshop because it was work of national importance. War experience has shewn us how high manual service stands in the grades of service which can be rendered for community interest. This new spirit does not appeal to force as a means of settling differences, nor to compulsory arbitration, nor to the authority of the State, nor to the power of organisation on either side. It is an appeal to reason, an approach to both sides to act in association on lines which will give freedom, self-respect, and security to both sides, whilst enabling each of them to submit to the other what it feels is best for the joint advancement of the trade and those engaged in it. In short, I would like to see inside the gates of every workshop the cultivation of the same spirit in British industry as has been hinted at already as the first essential for the future development of agriculture in England. Those processes of calling in the individual workman through committees, to which I will refer briefly in a moment, are not intended to take the place of the great organisations. They are to be supplementary to the Trade Unions, and are not intended to supplant them.

Trades Union leadership has changed hands to a great extent during the past year or two, and the virtual leaders of the men are now men themselves employed at the bench and in the mine. They are exercising very great authority and influence over masses of their fellow workmen, and often the authority, and decisions, and advice of executives and leaders are set aside and the advice of the men employed in the workshop, given to their fellow workmen as mates, is followed. So with this change, due to conditions into which we have not time to go, there must be recognised the need for applying new remedies in considering this question of improving the relations between employer and employed. It will not do now merely to have discussions between association and association. We might improve upon that and supplement it as I have said by having discussions direct in the workshop with the workmen themselves, who would be brought into touch at once with persons who were responsible for what action must be taken. So leadership having been to some extent transferred from the Trade Union to the workshop, the workman must be followed there and must be shewn how essential it is to recruit his good will and his aid in improving workshop conditions, not for the betterment of the management, but as much, if not more, for his own betterment as a workman in the shop. This may not touch certain industries in the country that are non-organised. Some of those trades, much to our shame, in former years were known as sweated industries, but even there it is found that the workers, men and women alike, are coming gradually into the trades unions, and should they not be in the trades unions to any great extent they are to be reached by other ways and means which this committee has developed. It is intended to apply to them, so as to establish the necessary machinery for better relations, the personnel of the Trades Boards Acts, those boards which, in the absence of trades unions, deal with the sweated conditions of thousands of workers employed in those sweated trades. So I have no fear myself of the non-organised trades being left altogether out of the range of the spirit to which I have referred. In addition to the committees there is to be in every district, it is proposed, a representative council, drawn from the employers and employed of the particular industry, and some scores of these councils are now being set up. In addition, there is to be in relation to every principal industry a national council, and many of us are now engaged in the creation of those several bodies. The public may not hear much about them, but they are the foundation upon which this structure of better relations is to rest, and, so far as we can spare some small margin of our time for those duties, considerable headway has been made in establishing these different organisations.

But I attach most importance to the workshop committees, and so I want to pursue this idea a little further. What are those committees to be? They would have to be free representative bodies, chosen by the men themselves. They could be empowered to meet the management, possessed of a sense of responsibility, to discuss in their own homely way matters which would have to be settled between them. Indeed, we know from experience that many of the big trade disputes in this country have grown out of trifles, out of small nothings comparatively, which could well have been settled inside the workshop gates by bringing master and man together, empowered to discuss matters which both understand as matters of personal experience. The committees when created, in this atmosphere and spirit to which I refer, would exist not in rebellion against the trade unions or against the trade union system, or exist as being in revolt against the management of the works, or the employer of labour. The committees would be vested with responsibility for negotiations. They would be able to use the personal knowledge derived from contact with the questions arising day by day. They would develop a sense of independence and a sense of just dealing, so that the doctrine of "a fair day's wage for a fair day's work" should apply not only to the wages but to the work to be done, a thing which sometimes does not occur. These committees could check the driving methods of some persons in authority, and, whilst getting the best from those who are above them, they could give the best, as I am sure they would provided the spirit is created, from the workmen in return for the fairer treatment they would enjoy. These committees could deal not only with manual service and ordinary work and wage questions; they could develop a better use of industrial capacity and technical knowledge in matters of workshop life.

But the spirit is everything, and the best desires of equitable workshop management could find expression through those committees if they were created. The committees would give a chance to the many workmen who now talk a great deal about democracy to express that democracy through the persons of the workmen themselves. I fear there are many of our friends in the labour movement, as we term it, who are given freely to talking of democracy without clearly understanding all that is covered in that term. It is a term which, it is a pleasure to see, has recently found its way not merely into the phrases of statesmen, but into the King's speech itself. We are now speaking commonly of all the sacrifices that are being made, of all the blood and treasure that is being spilt, in order to have a wholesome democratic system of world government. Well, we must begin in the workshops, for you cannot have peace on a large scale the country over, or between nation and nation, unless you have peace in our places of employment. They are the starting points and there it is that your contented millions must first be found. If they are not happy and if they are not at ease in connexion with their national service, you cannot expect any of those larger results for which highminded statesmen are seeking the world over.

Upon two main lines, in my judgment, democracy will require the most sane guidance and most sagacious advice which its leaders are capable of giving to it. It will not do for leaders merely to say that the future of the world must be decided, not by diplomats or thrones or Kaisers, but by the will of peoples. The will of peoples can find enduring and beneficial expression only when that will seeks social change by reasonable and calculated instalments, and not by any violent act of revolution. Peaceful voters on their way to the ballot boxes and properly formulated principles will in the end go further than fire and sword in the internal affairs of a nation. I say this because of the loose talk we have heard from many labour platforms recently of revolution and its benefits. Revolution may well be in any country the beginning and not the end of internal troubles, often expressed in a more painful and more violent form than ever. We need only look at our former great partner, Russia, to find full confirmation of all I have now implied. The red flag marches with the machine gun and the black cap when a certain stage of physical revolt is reached. The theory of new methods of life can only find rational application when democracy is wisely guided in taking slow but sure steps peacefully to turn its theories into an applied system, wherein the people of a nation and not merely a section or a class shall find their proper place and security for service, and find an assured existence under conditions of comfort for themselves and advantage to the State. Democratic leaders must tell these things to the people time after time if need be. They must repeat them so that the masses may understand them, because the tendency in labour has been to narrow the meaning of democracy. Democracy is not, and ought not to be, limited to those who now constitute the industrial population. Democracy is not a sect or a trade union club. Democracy is wider than the confines of the manual worker. Democracy should strive to reach the highest level of morality in doctrine and aspiration. It is not a class formula. It is a great and elevating faith which may be shared by all who believe in it. Democracy stands for the general progress of mankind and means the uplifting of men, and the liberation and unifying of nations. It does not mean the dominion of one class over another, nor the violent wresting of position or authority by some dramatic act of physical force, which if used would still leave a nation in a state of unreconciled and contending factions. Democracy, again, is a spirit whereby vast social and economic change may be effected through a medium approaching common consent or at least by the application of the political power of the people acting through representative institutions and resting upon ideas which majorities accept and understand. The spirit which has already accepted vast political changes can be made to apply to vast economic and industrial changes. This spirit must be cultivated by the leaders of democracy. They have now opportunities as great as their responsibilities. The success of parties, in the old sense of the term, is a trivial thing to the success of the great ends to be secured. These ends will justify the use of any constitutional means for dethroning that form of power upon which privilege and the mere possession of wealth have rested. But democracy must not be duped by phrases, nor be swayed by any influence which does not lead to a lasting advance for the nation as a whole. Nor should its leaders think that fundamental and enduring changes in our social system can be reached by any short cut to which the great mass of the people have not been converted. Progress will be faster in the future if impatience and folly do not retard it.

Having said a little with regard to the position of the poorer people, let me before I close respectfully address a few words to the richer and more favoured in the country. Should all rich folk in the country work? That is a very plain and I dare say it will be regarded in some

places as quite an impudent question. But really, rich
people who have never had cause in any way to earn
their living have always been a danger to the State, just
as they have been the greatest instance of wicked waste
to be found in any country. There is nothing more
melancholy, and even degrading, to a country than the
sight of educated people who have nothing to do. Wealth
is the fruit of service and endeavour. Work is the only
medium by which the ravages of the war can be made
good. Ignorance and idleness present a most pitiable
spectacle, but the most criminal of all sights is education
and idleness combined. Finally, let me say that whilst
I have addressed myself mainly in terms of appeal to the
workers, I am not unmindful at all of the difficulties of
the great employers of labour and those covered by the
phrase "our Captains of Industry." I know that many
of them work very hard under the greatest and most
trying mental pressure, and have duties and trials
unknown even to the workmen, but with those duties
and trials come reliefs again unknown to the workmen—
holidays, change, and rest, and the meeting of men of
their own class whose very company is an intellectual
joy, so that the worst off your employer of labour as a
human being may be he is far better off than the average
workman. Think of the housing conditions of so many
thousands, hundreds of thousands, of workmen, and how
intolerable it would be for you to live under those conditions, how discontented you would be, how discontented
the rich would be were it their fate to drag on an existence
in some of those places which are commonly described
by the term "houses." Why, the very waiting room of
the employer's ordinary office is a much more cosy and
pleasant place than the homes of many of the most

industrious workers of England. I plead that the elements
of the human order should begin to pervade the relations
of the workshop, that the workman should be less of a
drudge and more of a human asset than he has been,
that he should be brought into partnership in the under-
taking and in the management; that incidentally he
should have a more secure remuneration and not have
to bear the penalties and ordeals of employment as he
has had alone to bear them during times of trade depres-
sion and unemployment in previous years. The human
side of the workshop has, therefore, to be built up, and
you cannot hope to build it up upon any foundation of
drudgery such as the workmen in the main have had to
live under, and, as I have said, it will pay the country
to conciliate the men on these terms. It is a high ideal,
but it is attainable. I believe it is attainable because
we have seen it in another sphere of sacrifice where it has
already been secured. The war has brought all classes
together. In the trenches, at sea, and in all theatres of
danger, men of all classes are now labouring shoulder to
shoulder. There you have had a sinking of individual
interests. There you have had a common sacrifice, a
common endeavour for a common cause. Surely, as all
classes have been able to unite in their sacrifice and in
their resistance of the aggression of a foreign foe, it is,
I hope, not asking too much that when they come back
and take their places in peaceful pursuits again, and
become masters, workmen, managers, and foremen in
our enterprises and businesses, when they return from
danger and come back to take their places amongst us,—
surely it is not too much to hope that those who are able
to unite abroad will be able to unite for the ends of peace
and joy here at home.

UNITY IN THE EMPIRE

By F. J. CHAMBERLAIN, C.B.E.

THE word "unity" in relation to the Empire has a deeper meaning to-day than it had five years ago. Then it was a watchword, a theme for Imperial conferences and for speakers at demonstrations. The sanguine were sure, the pessimists and that great body of Britishers of moderate views and moderate faith regarded it as one of the things hoped for.

With dramatic suddenness the event clarified the situation, England awoke at war. There was no time for preliminary councils. The supreme test of the Empire had been reached. It is no exaggeration to say that the whole world watched with eagerness for the result. It was in that moment that the great discovery was made. The British Empire stood fast. From that day until now, from end to end of the world has been seen an object lesson of unity that has justified the sanguine, and been an inspiration to the Allies. That revelation has been more inspiring because the world is aware that it is in spite of the most sinister and subtle campaign against it, planned and brilliantly executed by an enemy under the cloak of friendship. I do not forget the tragic circumstances of one small nation within the Empire. But Ireland has given more evidence of her faithfulness to Empire on the fields of France and Flanders than of her treachery at home, and to-day we have more reason to count her ours than has the enemy. Examine the position in cold blood, if you can, and you are still aware of a substantial, solid, and effective unity running round the Empire, binding it in one as with a girdle of scarlet and gold.

The war is not responsible for the unity; it has only discovered or uncovered it. The storm does not establish foundations; it may reveal them. A century of building has created the structure that the storm has failed to destroy.

The British Empire is a successful experiment on the lines of the longed-for League of Nations. The race contains no more diverse elements than are found within its borders; one-third of the land surface of the world, and one-fifth of the inhabitants, have been held together in a living federation and have been kept until this day. Upon our generation rests the awful and splendid responsibility of proving to a questioning world that this unity can be made permanent, and of illustrating how a still larger unity may be achieved.

You will forgive one or two homely pictures of our unity that cannot fail to strike the imagination. It has been our privilege to meet thousands of men from the Overseas Dominions. How many times have boys, whose forefathers emigrated from England or Scotland, who were themselves born in Australia, or on the Western plains of Canada, said, "I have been wanting to come *home* all my life"? These islands are the "home" of the Empire, and there is no more wonderful word in the language.

Or think of Botha and Smuts, within the memory almost of the youngest of us, fighting with all their heart

and mind against the Empire, and, to-day, dominant
personalities proclaiming their loyalty, and proving it in
unrivalled service.

Or picture, if you can, young India, pouring out her
life-blood with pride and ready sacrifice, in France, in
Egypt, and in Mesopotamia, for the "British Raj." The
most moving scene in the history of the British Commons
was on that evening in 1915, when the princes of India
stood amidst the representatives of the people of the
homelands and paid their homage.

How much such things mean will depend on the vision
of those who hear them; but they have in them the stuff
that holds the future.

This ghastly war, not of our choosing, has transferred
the seats of learning for young Britain from their peaceful
sites to the battlefield. If the object of education is the
cultivation of the power of thought and observation, the
kindling of imagination, and the extension of knowledge;
then "over there" is a University set in full array, with
ghostly as well as human tutors, a curriculum without
precedent, and such a body of undergraduates as Cambridge or Oxford might covet.

It is not for nothing, as regards the Empire, that your
sons, the children of the East End, and the boys of
Canada, Australasia, and South Africa, are meeting and
mingling with Gurkha and Sikh, and with each other.
They are sharing a common discipline, a common adven-
ture, making sacrifice together. They are seeing each
other with eyes from which the scales are falling, and
knowledge and understanding are growing out of their
contact. The farthest reaches of Empire have been
brought nearer to the Empire's heart by this brotherhood

in arms, and the barriers between classes have been lowered until a man can step across them without climbing. The distance between East and West has been immeasurably shortened, whether we are thinking in terms of London, or of the Empire.

In our consideration of this whole subject we are to take the Christian standpoint. To us, the words "Thy Kingdom come on earth as it is in Heaven," on Divine lips were more than a pious wish. They were a great intention, the expression of age-long purpose. We believe that the gains of the centuries—the harvest of the past which is worth conserving—have been secured by moral and spiritual conquest, rather than by military or political achievement. There may be elements in our present forms of unity which we may well allow to go by the board. The things that make for permanence will abide not only with an enlightened statesmanship, but with a growing understanding, an ever broadening interpretation of Christian teaching about

> The Kingdom of God on earth,
> The Universal Fatherhood of God, and
> The brotherhood of man,

leading the nation to see that the knowledge of God and of His Christ is the rightful inheritance of every son of the Empire.

As these great ideals of social life have been interpreted in the life of either sovereign peoples or subject peoples, so, we believe, and only so, have bonds been forged that can be trusted to stand the strain which time and changing condition and circumstances impose.

Unity, even the Empire itself ultimately, depends, as we believe, on a broad-based statesmanship, carrying up the main principles of our Government to their highest power in action, and, constantly throughout the Empire, mediating those doctrines to the peoples concerned as they are able to bear them, with ever-extending inspiration and encouragement to growth and development.

Our Imperial aims are neither antagonistic to nor inconsistent with our Christian programme. That should constitute a challenge to the Christian Churches, and is in itself a matter for high and solemn pride. The war has cleared the air. As stated during this period, the ideal of a federation of nations, free, independent, and at the same time interdependent, each working out its national destiny, each contributing, in terms of opportunity, to the well-being of the whole, bringing to bear on Imperial matters the heart, brain, will of the whole, gives us a picture of a Commonwealth in advance of any contemporary political programme, with the one conspicuous exception of that of the United States of America, between whom and ourselves is being established a Unity which may well be more valuable to the world at large and to ourselves than any formal Union.

Here, as we see it, is our opportunity. The Christian forces of the Empire have the onus of maintaining the national outlook at this high level. Our faith, our audacity, our leadership will be needed if lesser counsels are to have no chance of prevailing. There must be no swing of the pendulum back to smaller views.

With the coming of Peace, the temptation to the Nation to take off its armour, to come down from the pedestal, to revert to pre-war conditions, to re-act in self-indulgence from the strain of war, or to let materialism defeat idealism, will be well-nigh overwhelming. To give way to that temptation will be to rob victory of any permanent values. It will be a poor thing to have taught Germany her lesson, if we fail to learn our own.

We see no hope of successful resistance of that temptation apart from the mobilisation of the Christian forces within the Empire into an army committed to the sacred task of making the conscience of the Nation effectively Christian, leading the way in bringing about a closer approximation between the politics of the State and the programme of the Kingdom of God, and proclaiming that Kingdom at hand.

If we are agreed so far it behoves us to look for the practical implications of the position. These islands are still the heart and home of the Empire. This was the rock whence its younger peoples were hewn. Our nation has produced the men and the machinery that govern our commonwealth. The lonely places, farthest removed from us, will be peopled largely by and through the work of children of the Old Country. There, wherever her children go, is England.

England is a treasure house, where the very stones are eloquent. Her history, her buildings, her national and civic life, her denominations and movements are all of them of vital interest to her children. It is a place of pilgrimage and remembrance. It is more. They find here the mature growths from which their institutions have sprung. They love our historic places, they love our crowded cities, they love our seashores and our quiet country-side, for everywhere they go they find not only the story of our past, but that of their own. This is their spiritual home. Our art, our literature, our movements are parts of a common inheritance, and it is the pride of

the Motherland that her children have never outgrown
their love of the old home, their veneration for its sanctions and restraints, and that on their own homesteads
they have reproduced in new settings and often in fresh
forms so much that is native here.

One would like to see a larger share in this priceless
inheritance offered to our peoples oversea. Think for one
moment of our great Cathedrals, unique and wonderful.
They can never be reproduced. They might be copied;
but Canterbury and Westminster, Lincoln and Durham,
York and the rest would still remain all that they are to
us and to them. You cannot transplant history. In the
homeland we are but trustees of these treasures, and we
ought to make them the home and centre of our Imperial
Christianity. In every one of them the priests of the
Church in the Overseas lands should not only be seen
but heard. Is there no room in Cathedral Chapters for
Overseas representatives, so that in our daily services
in a new and living way we may be linked together in
sacrament, praise and prayer, and in the proclamation of
Christian truth? One Canonry for each historic building
would mean more to Unity than many resolutions at
Congress. Perhaps that is as far as one ought to go in
suggestion, but there are other splendid possibilities that
one would love to discuss. No one thinking of Unity in
the Empire can fail to rejoice in the growing desire
manifest among Christian Denominations for Unity. I
will not trench on another's subject beyond saying that
the way to Union is Unity, and that it would be tragic
if in these momentous days any stone was left unturned
that would lead to better knowledge, deeper understanding
and sympathy between those who name the Name that

is above every name. And our people overseas have much
to teach us in this matter. Over great areas of social
opportunity and service the Catholic Church may act
unitedly and must do so, if she is to enter on offensive
warfare and not stand for another generation on the
defensive. The war has made a difference here. Men, who
in the conventional days of peace rarely met, have
joined hands in service. Catholic and Protestant, Churchman and Free Churchman, have found joy in fellowship.
That does not mean that differences have disappeared, it
means that, recognising and estimating their differences,
it has been possible to establish a basis of co-operation,
in knowledge, understanding, and sympathy, and to
recognise in one another the hall-mark of Christian faith
and character. Is this to be a war measure only? or is it
to be one of the great gains to be carried over into the
days ahead?

One other question clamours for treatment: the problem of the evangelisation of the Empire. Christianity
must be given its chance in every corner of the Empire.
There may be divergent opinions as to the methods to
be used, but if Christianity contains in its gospel the
pearl of great price, there can be no two opinions as to
the obligation that rests on us to bring to the nations
federated with us this supreme gift. Nothing can release
us from that responsibility. To postpone the presentation
of the Christian gospel for any of the time-honoured
excuses:

(1) our pre-occupation in matters of more urgent
importance elsewhere,

(2) any fear of the effects of Christianity on our political
or commercial interests,

(3) the desire to live down prejudice and establish confidence,

(4) the preparation of a people's mind by education before introducing a new religion,
—any one of these is treachery to the All-Father and to the family of man, and a vital *praeparatio evangelica* is being made. Let me illustrate.

It happened in a great marquee in France. On a summer evening in 1916 the place was crowded with Indians. There was a group playing Indian card games, there was a crowd round a gramophone with Indian records, at the writing tables with great torment of spirit men were writing to their homes. At the counter foods they loved were being provided. Against one of the poles of the marquee stood a stately Indian of some rank. He had been seen there often before. He rarely spoke but seemed intensely interested. On this particular night the time arrived for the closing of the tent. The little groups gradually disappeared and the tent curtains were being replaced when the leader of the work found himself addressed by the Indian:

Why do you serve us in this way? You are not here by Government orders. You come when you like and you go when you like. There is only one religion on earth that would lead its servants to serve in this way, Christianity. I have been watching you men, and I have come to the conclusion that Christianity will fit the East as it can never fit the West. When the war is over I want you to send one of your men to my village. We are all Hindus, but my people will do what I tell them.

One of the ghastly tragedies of the war is that two great nations nominally Christian are at each other's throats. In the world's eyes Christian civilisation has broken down. We know better, but our explanations will not carry far enough to correct the impression. Our defence must be an offensive.

It is certainly within the truth to say that we have not yet seen what Christianity can do for a community or a nation where, as I put it before, "it is given a chance." May it not be that in the Providence of God the first great revelation of what Christianity can do for à nation will be seen in one of the lands that have come under the Flag, and among a people living under less complex conditions than ourselves? If that is a possibility we ought to see that wherever the Flag flies, there comes, with the unfurling of the Flag, the Gospel of Christ.

This is directly in the interest of unity, and many problems that have so far remained insoluble to our statesmen might discover the solution in Christian leadership.

I shall be pardoned I know for suggesting that the highest purposes of unity may be served by the extension and development throughout the Empire of such international organisations as the Student Christian Movement, the Y.M.C.A., the Y.W.C.A., and, used at its highest values, the Boy Scout Movement. There are others, but these are typical. They are established movements built up on definite principles capable of universal application, and yet each of them able to develop its organisation on lines that recognise national psychology and character. Each of them may become and aims at becoming indigenous everywhere, giving freedom of method and action and free play to the moral and intellectual activities of the people concerned, while they have certain essential elements that are universally characteristic of them. In addition, they give large numbers of Christian people an opportunity of expressing their unity in service of the right kind.

What was said about the Cathedrals is equally true of our two ancient Universities. Mr Fisher's Education Bill may well mean more for Imperial unity than almost any other single factor. It will mean an ever increasing number of men to whom "Cambridge" and "Oxford" will be magic words. If our view of culture is broad enough we shall see to it that these two Universities become increasingly places where the children of the Empire who are fit to graduate in them shall not lack the opportunity of doing so. Because these ancient foundations link with the past, because of all they may mean to the present and to the future, the way to them should be made broad enough to admit the living stream of Greater Britain's children, who by dint of gifts and industry have proved their fitness to meet their peers in these delectable cities, where the very air breathes the romance of British culture. Their right of entry ought not to be won by the bene-factions of private citizens, though all who love knowledge are grateful enough for these, but should be theirs by their citizenship in the Empire and their own tested fitness.

Nothing again is more hopeful in the present situation than the manifest desire, widely felt and expressed, that the old class-antagonisms should never be revived. Surely this is *the* strategic moment in which we may make the War once more contribute to a better state of things. Our politicians are awake to the need and are inventing every kind of machinery for bringing Capital and Labour together in Council Chambers as co-partners in the Com-merce of the Empire. But there are sinister forces also at work, and this machinery can only run if it is controlled by men of resolute good will.

The War has been a great bridge builder linking up in the fellowship of discipline and sacrifice people between whom chasms yawned before. There are knowledge and understanding and sympathy to-day amongst us. Yet many of us are convinced that no purely political machinery can be made effective in achieving so great a task as the making permanent of this new and better condition. We need a new and abiding spirit of conciliation, a deeper determination than political action can produce, that things shall not relapse, that the forces of re-action shall not triumph. The one hope of carrying over into permanence this new understanding and appreciation lies in the nation becoming impregnated with those spacious spiritual ideals that the Churches together represent. Nothing is impossible to faith, and faith in God and man will be kept astretch in the discipline that will be demanded of us all, in the breaking down of false barriers that have grown up through the years and the destruction of long-lived prejudices that will die hard.

The Empire itself is a unity. It is not easy for English people to realise all that is implied here. My great namesake urged us in this country to "think Imperially." Another voice asks us "What do they know of England who only England know?" but it is hard for us to think except in terms of England. For example, I have referred to this country as the great treasure house of the Empire's history, and to the care and devotion shewn by our kinsmen from Overseas in their study of our country and its institutions. All of us realise how right that is, but ought we not to reciprocate their devotion and regard, by much more intense interest and study of their life and the developments of their institutions?

Our unity demands this wider culture, this reciprocity. The Motherland must not only teach, she must be prepared to learn. She may lead, but she must be prepared to follow. We have much to contribute, but in Religion, in political and social ideals, and in commerce there is much we need to receive.

If our land is the great treasure house, are not these other lands great laboratories where we might see, if we would only look, how some of our accepted ideas, and notions, and watchwords are tested in a larger arena?

Are we so sure of ourselves that we are prepared to hold on to our own experience as the final test of the truth and value of our theories? Or are we big enough in the light of Imperial experience to revise our judgment, to sift our theories, and to go forward carrying those which stand the test of the wider arena, and being prepared to surrender those which only seemed right and proper in the conventional setting of these small islands?

In conclusion, the Empire has come to power and unity on certain great principles. Our Imperial ideals have been evolved out of experience all over the world, and with all kinds of people, under the guidance of distinguished leaders of many-sided gifts. In an Empire so diverse in its constituent parts, including peoples at varied stages of development, it is impossible that those ideals should be everywhere expressed at their highest power. In many places our methods of government must be tentative, but everywhere they must be progressive, placing upon subject peoples the burden of government as rapidly as they are able to bear it, providing every inspiration that can call them upwards and onwards. Our tentative methods must never be allowed to become permanent. We may be tutors, we must never become tyrants. We may lead, direct, even control, but we may never be content until our people are free, self-governing, rejoicing in the liberty that enables them to choose whole-heartedly to remain in that Commonwealth of free peoples we call the Empire. Along this path lie permanence and closer unity. In our Imperial destiny it is the part of those who would be the greatest to become the servants of all.

Thank God for all who have laboured in this spirit to build our goodly heritage.

UNITY BETWEEN NATIONS

By the Rev. J. H. B. Masterman, M.A.

In the previous lectures of this course you have been considering the problem of home reunion. My task to-day is to remind you of the fact that beyond the reunion of the Churches at home there lies the larger problem of the realisation of the Christian ideal of a universal brotherhood. How can this ideal be realised in a world divided into nations? I am going to treat the subject historically; firstly because I find myself incapable of treating it in any other way, and secondly because you can only build securely if you build on the foundation of the historic past. The State may ignore the lessons of the past, the Church can never do so.

How can we deal with the apparent antagonism between the centrifugal force of nationality and the centripetal force of the Catholic ideal? There are two possible answers that we cannot accept. It is possible for religion to set itself against the development of national life, and claim that a world-religion must find expression in a world-state. That is the mediaeval answer.

Or it is possible for religion to become subordinate to nationality at the cost of losing the note of Catholicity, so that the consecration of national life may seem a nobler task than the gathering of humanity into conscious fellowship in one great society. This is the modern answer.

With neither of these solutions can we be satisfied. The existence of nations as units of political self-consciousness within the larger life of humanity does, we believe, minister to the fulfilment of the purpose of God. Whatever may be the case hereafter, the establishment of a world-state, at the present stage in the evolution of human institutions, would mean the impoverishment of the life of humanity. Yet a Church that is merely national or imperial has missed the true significance of its mission.

At the beginning of the Christian era, the greatest attempt ever made to gather all peoples into a universal society was actually in progress. The Roman Empire was founded on the basis of a common administrative system, and a common law—the *jus gentium*. It needed a common religion. The effort to supply this passes through three stages. The earliest of these is the stage of universal toleration which was made possible by polytheism. A second stage soon follows. The various religions of the Empire overflow one another's frontier-lines and a synthesis begins, leading to the Stoic idea of the universal truth expressed in many forms. But the popular mind was unable to rise to this high conception, and the third stage begins towards the end of the first century in the formal adoption of the worship of the Emperor as the religious expression of the unity of the Empire. It was the opposition of the Christian Church that did most to bring to naught this effort to give a religious foundation to the unity of the Empire, and the attempt of Constantine and Theodosius to make Christianity an Imperial religion came too late to save the Empire from disintegration.

For the unity of the Christian Church had been undermined. When Christianity shook itself free from the shackles of Jewish nationalism, it came under the influence of Greek thought. The theology and language of the early Church were Greek. Even in Rome the Church was for at least two centuries "a Greek colony." Hence the growth of Christianity was slow in those western parts of the Empire that had not come under the influence of Greek culture—Gaul, Britain, Spain, North Africa. Latin Christianity found its centre in North Africa, where Roman culture had imposed itself on the hard, cruel Carthaginian world. It is Carthage, not Athens, that gives to Tertullian his harsh intolerance and to St Augustine his stern determinism. So the way was prepared for what I regard as the supreme tragedy of history—the falling apart of Eastern and Western Christianity. Then, in the West, the unity of the Church is broken by the conversion of the Teutonic peoples to Arianism, so that the contest between the dying Empire in the West and the tribes pressing on its frontiers is embittered by religious antagonism. The sword of Clovis secured the victory of orthodoxy, but at what a cost!

When the storm subsides, there emerges the august conception of the Holy Roman Empire. For the noblest expression of the ideal of a universal Christian Empire, read Dante's *De Monarchia*. The history of the Holy Roman Empire is too large a subject to enter upon. It is important to remember that the struggles between the Popes and the Emperors that fill so large a space of mediaeval history were not struggles between Church and State. Western Europe was conceived of as one Christian Society—an attempt to realise the City of God of St Augustine's great treatise—and the question at issue was whether the Pope or the Emperor was to be regarded as the supreme head of this great society.

The unity of Western Christendom found a crude, but real, expression in the Crusades, and it is significant that the decline of the crusading impulse coincides in time with the rise of national feeling in the two western states, England and France. What was to be the attitude of the Catholic Church towards this new national instinct? In the 14th and 15th centuries the question becomes increasingly urgent, and the Council of Constance may be regarded as the last sincere effort to find an answer. The answer suggested there, to which the English Church still adheres, was the recognition of a General Council of the Church as the supreme spiritual authority. Such a General Council might gather the glory and honour of the nations into the City of God, and might even, it was hoped, restore the broken unity between East and West. How the Council failed, how Constantinople was left to its fate, how a Papacy growing more and more Italian in its interests brought to a head the long-simmering revolt of the nations—all this you know. The Reformation was, in part, a struggle of the nations to give religious expression to their national life. The threefold bond that had held together the Church of the West—the bond of common language, law and cere-monial—was broken.

At the threshold of the new order stand the figures of Luther and Machiavelli, as champions of the supremacy of the State. True, Luther thinks of the State as a Christian society, while Machiavelli is the father of the modern German doctrine of the non-moral character of state action. But the Augsburg compromise, *cujus regio, ejus religio*, was a frank subordination of the Church to secular authority. The Tudor sovereigns adopted the doctrine with alacrity, and imposed on the Church of England a subjection to secular authority from which it has not yet been able to disentangle itself.

While Lutheranism tended to treat religion as a department of the State, Calvinism claimed for the Church an authority that threatened the very existence of the State. Calvinism represents the second attempt to give practical expression to St Augustine's *Civitas Dei*, as the Holy Roman Empire was the first. It failed, in part, because it lost its catholic character, and became (as, for example, in Scotland) intensely national. The disintegration of the Catholic Church in the West was helped by two influences. The first was the return to the standards and ideals of the Old Testament. The appeal of the reformers to Holy Scripture involved the elevation of the Old Testament to the same level of authority as the New. The crude nationalism of Judaism obscured the Christian idea of a universal brotherhood—St Paul's secret hidden from the foundation of the world, to be revealed in the fulness of time in the Christian gospel. Even now we hardly realise how largely our ideas of religion are derived from the imperfect moral standards of the Old Testament. The other influence was the identification of the Papacy with the Antichrist of the Book of Revelation—the Protestant answer to the Roman excommunication of heretics. The idea of a common Christianity deeper than all national antagonisms hardly existed in the Europe of the later half of the 16th century.

Nearly a century of wars of religion was followed by

seventy years of war in which the national idea played the leading part. The internationalism of the 18th century was a reaction against both religion and nationality. The Napoleonic struggle, and the Romantic revival, with its appeal to the past, re-awakened the national instinct. In France, Spain, Russia, Prussia, and Eastern Europe, national self-consciousness was stirred into life. In Russia and Spain, and among the Balkan peoples, this national awakening took a definitely religious character. But it was Italy that produced the one thinker to whom the real significance of nationality was revealed. Mazzini recognised, more clearly than any other political teacher of the time, how Nationalism founded on religion might lead to the brotherhood of nations in a world "made safe for democracy." The last century has been an epoch of exaggerated national self-consciousness. Against the aggressive tendencies of the greater nations, the smaller nations strove to protect themselves. Italy, Poland, Bohemia, Serbia, Greece, strove with varying degrees of success to achieve national self-expression. Nation strove with nation in a series of contests, of which the present war is the culmination.

The influence of Christianity was impotent to prevent war; though it was able to do something to restrain its worst excesses. Where the centrifugal force of nationality comes into opposition to the centripetal force of the Christian ideal, it is generally the former that wins. How is this impotence to be accounted for? Four reasons at least may be noted. (1) The "inwardness" of Lutheranism, combined with the cynicism of the Machiavellian doctrine of the non-moral character of public policy led, especially in Germany, to an entire disregard of the principles of

Christianity in the public policy of the State. Nations did not even profess to be guided by Christian principles in their dealings with each other. The noble declaration of Alexander I remained a piece of "sublime nonsense" to statesmen like Metternich and Castlereagh, and their successors. (2) The internal life of the nations was, and is, only partially Christianised. Nations cannot regulate their external policy on Christian principles unless those principles are accepted as authoritative in their internal affairs. (3) The influence of Christianity has been hindered, to a degree difficult to exaggerate, by the unhappy divisions that, especially in England and in the United States, have made it impossible for the Church to speak with a united voice. (4) The idea of the Sovereignty of the State and its supreme claim on the life of the individual, with which Dr Figgis has dealt with illuminating insight in his *Churches in the Modern State*, has prevented the idea of the Churches as local expressions of a universal society from exercising the corrective influence that it ought to exercise on the over-emphasis of State independence.

The State is only one of the various forms in which national life expresses itself. It is the nation organised for self-protection. And wherever self-protection becomes the supreme need, the State, like Aaron's rod, swallows all the rest. But in many directions, the world has become, or is becoming, international. Science and philosophy, and, to a lesser degree, theology and art, have become the common possession of all civilised nations. The effort to make commerce the expression of international fellowship, with which the name of Cobden is associated, failed, largely as the result of the German policy of high tariffs, but its defeat is only temporary, and the commercial interdependence of nations will reassert its influence when the present phase of international strife is over. The function of the Church is to express the common life and interests of nations, as the State expresses the distinctive character of each. So the Church holds to the four universal things—the authority of Holy Scripture; the Creeds; the two Sacraments, and the historic episcopate. We believe that the retention of the historic Episcopate is essential to the maintenance of the Catholic ideal of the Church. For the bishop is the link between the local and the universal Church; the representative and guardian of the Catholic ideal in the life of the local community; and the representative of the local community in the counsels of the Catholic Church. I have often wished that at least one bishop from some other Church than our own could be associated with the consecration of all bishops of the Anglican Church. For by such association we should bring into clearer prominence the fact that the historic episcopate is more than a national institution.

So we reach the final question: What can the Churches do to promote the unity of the nations?

An invitation was recently issued by the Archbishop of Upsala for a conference of representatives of the Christian Churches, to reassert, even in this day of disunion, the essential unity of the Body of Christ. For various reasons, such a conference at the present juncture seems impracticable, but the time may come when, side by side with a Congress of the nations, a gathering of representatives of the Churches may be called together to reinforce, by its witness, the idea of international fellowship.

For a League of Churches might well prepare the way for a League of Nations. Such a League of Churches would naturally find expression in a permanent Advisory Council—a kind of ecclesiastical Hague tribunal. Historical antagonisms seem to preclude the selection of Rome or Constantinople as the place of meeting of this Council. Surely there is no other place so suited for the purpose as Jerusalem. Here the appointed representatives of all the Churches, living in constant intercourse with one another, might draw together the severed parts of the One Body, till the glory and honour of the nations find, even in the earthly Jerusalem, their natural centre and home. Thus, and thus only, can the spiritual foundation for a League of Nations be well and truly laid.

Two things are involved in any such scheme for a League of Churches. No one Church must claim a paramount position or demand submission as the price of fellowship; and all excommunications of one Church by another must be swept away.

Christ did not come to destroy the local loyalties that lift human life out of selfish isolation. These loyalties only become anti-Christian when they become exclusive. The early loyalty of primitive man to his family or clan was deemed to involve a normal condition of antagonism to neighbouring families or clans. Turn a page of history, and tribal loyalty has become civic loyalty. But civic loyalty, as in the cities of Greece or Italy or Flanders, involves intermittent hostility with neighbouring cities. Then civic loyalty passes into national loyalty, and again patriotism expresses itself in distrust and antipathy to other nations. And this will also be so till we see that all these local loyalties rest on the foundation of a deeper loyalty to the Divine ideal of universal fellowship that found its supreme expression in the Incarnation and its justification in the truth that God so loved the world.

To the Christian man national life can never be an end in itself but always a means to an end beyond itself. A nation exists to serve the cause of humanity; by what it gives, not by what it gets, will its worth be estimated at the judgment-bar of God.

"Whoso loveth father or mother more than me is not worthy of me" must have seemed a hard saying to those to whom it was first spoken; and "whoso loveth city or fatherland more than me is not worthy of me" may seem a hard saying to us to-day; yet nothing less than this is involved in our pledge of loyalty to Christ. Christian patriotism never found more passionate expression than in St Paul's wish that he might be anathema for the sake of his nation; yet passionately as he loved his own people, he loved with a deeper passion the Catholic Church within which there was neither Jew nor Greek, Barbarian, Scythian, bond nor free. It is because the idea of the Catholic Church has become to the majority of Christian people a matter of intellectual assent rather than of passionate conviction that the Church seems impotent in international affairs.

The last four centuries of European history have had as their special characteristic the development of nations. It may be that after this war we shall pass into a new era. The special feature of the period now closing has been the insecurity of national life. Menaced with constant danger, every nation has tended to develop an exaggerated self-consciousness that was liable to become inflamed and over-sensitive. If adequate security can be provided, by a League of Nations, or in some other way, for the free development of the national life of every nation, the senseless over-emphasis of nationality from which the past has suffered will no longer hinder the growth of a true Internationalism. I believe that the real alternative lies not between Nationality and Internationalism but between an Internationalism founded, like that of the 18th century, on non-Christian culture and materialism, and an Internationalism founded on the consecration of all the local loyalties that bind a man to family, city and nation, lifting him through local spheres of service to the service of the whole human race for whom Christ died. The tree whose leaves are for the healing of the nations grows only in the City of God. The Christian forces in the world are impotent to guide the future, because they are entangled in the present. Yet it is in the Holy Catholic Church that the one hope for humanity lies. It may be that that hope will never be realised; that the Holy Catholic Church is destined to remain to the end an unachieved ideal. But it is by unachieved ideals that men and nations live; and what matters most for every Christian man is that he should keep the Catholic mind and heart that reach out through home and city and country to all mankind, and rejoice that every man has an equal place in the impartial love of God.

For EU product safety concerns, contact us at Calle de José Abascal, 56–1°,
28003 Madrid, Spain or eugpsr@cambridge.org.

www.ingramcontent.com/pod-product-compliance
Ingram Content Group UK Ltd.
Pitfield, Milton Keynes, MK11 3LW, UK
UKHW012332130625
459647UK00009B/229